M000291177

Words to be spoken by men and women alike:

"I am the word that purifies,
I am the shining spirit of Ra, the Glorious Light,
I am the soul of Ra, the word!"

Cruzian Mystic Books / Sema Institute of Yoga
P.O.Box 570459
Miami, Florida, 33257
(305) 378-6253 Fax: (305) 378-6253

© 2000-2008 By Reginald Muata Abhaya Ashby

All rights reserved. No part of this book may be used or reproduced in any manner whatsoever without written permission (address above) except in the case of brief quotations embodied in critical articles and reviews. All inquiries may be addressed to the address above.

The author is available for group lectures and individual counseling. For further information contact the publisher.

Ashby, Muata
The Glorious Light Meditation ISBN: 1-884564-15-1

Library of Congress Cataloging in Publication Data

1 Meditation, 2 Ancient Egyptian Literature, 3 Self Help.

## Also by Muata Ashby

*Egyptian Yoga: The Philosophy of Enlightenment*
*Initiation Into Egyptian Yoga: The Secrets of Sheti*
*Egyptian Proverbs: Tempt Tchaas,*
*Mystical Wisdom Teachings and Meditations*
*The Egyptian Yoga Exercise Workout Book*
*Mysticism of Ushet Rekhat: Worship of the Divine Mother*

For more listings see the back section. Or visit these web sites:

www.GloriousLightMeditation.org
www.Egyptianyoga.com

# Sema
# Sema Institute of Yoga

Sema (⟊) is an ancient Egyptian word and symbol meaning *union*. The Sema Institute is dedicated to the propagation of the universal teachings of spiritual evolution which relate to the union of humanity and the union of all things within the universe. It is a non-denominational organization which recognizes the unifying principles in all spiritual and religious systems of evolution throughout the world. Our primary goals are to provide the wisdom of ancient spiritual teachings in books, courses and other forms of communication. Secondly, to provide expert instruction and training in the various yogic disciplines including Ancient Egyptian Philosophy, Christian Gnosticism, Indian Philosophy and modern science. Thirdly, to promote world peace and Universal Love.

A primary focus of our tradition is to identify and acknowledge the yogic principles within all religions and to relate them to each other in order to promote their deeper understanding as well as to show the essential unity of purpose and the unity of all living beings and nature within the whole of existence.

The Institute is open to all who believe in the principles of peace, non-violence and spiritual emancipation regardless of sex, race, or creed.

Sema Institute
P.O. Box 570459, Miami, Fla. 33257 (305) 378-6253,
Fax (305) 378-6253
©1997-2008

## About the author and editor:
## Dr. Muata Abhaya Ashby

Mr. Ashby began studies in the area of religion and philosophy and achieved a doctorate degree in these areas while at the same time he began to collect his research into what would later become several books on the subject of the African History, religion and ethics, world mythology, origins of Yoga Philosophy and practice in ancient Africa (Ancient Egypt/Nubia) and also the origins of Christianity in Ancient Egypt. This was the catalyst for a successful book series on the subject called "Egyptian Yoga" begun in 1994. He has extensively studied mystical religious traditions from around the world and is an accomplished lecturer, musician, artist, poet, painter, screenwriter, playwright and author of over 50 books on yoga philosophy, religious philosophy and social philosophy based on ancient African principles. A leading advocate of the concept of the existence of advanced social and religious philosophy in ancient Africa comparable to the Eastern traditions such as Vedanta, Buddhism, Confucianism and Taoism, he has lectured and written extensively on the correlations of these with ancient African religion and philosophy.

Muata Abhaya Ashby holds a Doctor of Divinity Degree from the American Institute of Holistic Theology and a Masters degree in Liberal Arts and Religious Studies from Thomas Edison State College. He has performed extensive researched Ancient Egyptian philosophy and social order as well as Maat philosophy, the ethical foundation of Ancient Egyptian society. In recent years he has researched the world economy in the last 300 years, focusing on the United States of America and western culture in general. He is also a Teacher of Yoga Philosophy and Discipline. Dr. Ashby is an adjunct professor at the American Institute of Holistic Theology and worked as an adjunct professor at the Florida International University.

Dr. Ashby has been an independent researcher and practitioner of Egyptian Yoga, Indian Yoga, Chinese Yoga, Buddhism and mystical psychology as well as Christian Mysticism. Dr. Ashby has engaged in Post Graduate research in advanced Jnana, Bhakti and Kundalini Yogas at the Yoga Research Foundation.

Since 1999 he has researched Ancient Egyptian musical theory and created a series of musical compositions which explore this unique area of music from ancient Africa and its connection to world music. Dr. Ashby has lectured around the United States of America, Europe and Africa.

Through his studies of the teachings of the great philosophers of the world and meeting with and studying under spiritual masters and having practiced advanced meditative disciplines, Dr. Ashby began to function in the capacity of Sebai or Spiritual Preceptor of Shetaut Neter, Ancient Egyptian Religion and also as Ethics Philosopher and Religious Studies instructor. Thus his title is Sebai and the acronym of his Kemetic and western names is MAA. He believes that it is important to understand all religious teachings in the context of human historical, cultural and social development in order to promote greater understanding and the advancement of humanity.

# Table of Contents

## TABLE OF FIGURES

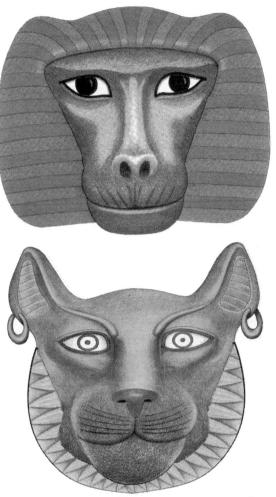

Above: Masks of Lord Djehuty [Djehuti] and Hetheru as the Lioness Goddess Sekhmit

GLORIOUS LIGHT MEDITATION

9

# INTRODUCTION: *Ra Akhu,* The Glorious Light, First Formal Meditation in History

## Ancient Meditation For Modern Times

The art of Meditation is a Yoga discipline which was practiced in Ancient Egypt for the purpose of promoting spiritual enlightenment. While it is not a religion, it is a tool used by religious and non-religious spiritual seekers to go within, to discover Higher Consciousness. This booklet presents the Kemetic (Ancient Egyptian) teachings related to the practice of meditation. Yoga is the practice of mental, physical and spiritual disciplines which lead to self-control and self-discovery by purifying the mind, body and spirit, so as to discover the deeper spiritual essence which lies within every human being and object in the universe. In essence, the goal of yoga practice is to unite or *yoke* one's individual consciousness with universal or cosmic consciousness. Therefore, Ancient Egyptian religious practice, especially in terms of the rituals and other practices of the Ancient Egyptian temple system known as *Shetaut Neter* (the way of the hidden Supreme Being), may be termed as a yoga system: *Egyptian Yoga*. In this sense, religion, in its purest form, is a yoga system, as it seeks to reunite people with their true and original source.

The disciplines of Yoga fall under five major categories. These are: *Yoga of Wisdom, Yoga of Devotional Love, Yoga of Meditation, Tantric Yoga* and *Yoga of Selfless Action.* Within these categories there are subsidiary forms which are part of the main disciplines. The emphasis in the Osirian Myth is on the Yoga of Wisdom, Yoga of Devotional Love and Yoga of Selfless Action. The important point to remember is that all aspects of yoga can and should be used in an integral fashion to effect an efficient and harmonized spiritual movement in the practitioner. Therefore, while there may be an area of special emphasis, other elements are bound to become part of the yoga program as needed. For example, while a yogin may place emphasis on the Yoga of Wisdom, they may also practice Devotional Yoga and Meditation Yoga along with the wisdom studies. So the practice of any discipline that leads to oneness with Supreme Consciousness can be called yoga. If you study, rationalize and reflect upon the teachings, you are practicing *Yoga of Wisdom.* If you meditate upon the teachings and your Higher Self, you are practicing *Yoga of Meditation.*

If you practice rituals which identify you with your spiritual nature, you are practicing *Yoga of Ritual Identification* (which is part of the Yoga of Wisdom and the Yoga of Devotional Love of the Divine). If you develop your physical nature and psychic energy centers, you are practicing *Serpent Power (Kundalini or Uraeus) Yoga* (which is part of Tantric Yoga). If you practice living according to the teachings of ethical behavior and selflessness, you are practicing *Yoga of Action* (Maat) in daily life. If you practice turning your attention towards the Divine by developing love for the Divine, then it is called *Devotional Yoga* or *Yoga of Divine Love.* The practitioner of yoga is called a yogin (male practitioner) or yogini (female practitioner), and one who has attained the culmination of yoga (union with the Divine) is called a yogi. In this manner, yoga has been developed into many disciplines which may be used in an integral fashion to achieve the same goal: Enlightenment. And essentially, anyone who has achieved this level of higher consciousness can be described as a "Yogi" regardless of whatever path they used (Egyptian, Indian, Chinese, etc.) to attain that Enlightenment. However, in the case of the Egyptian practice we have a term, *Sema,* that is actually the same in meaning as the familiar term "Yoga" of India. Therefore, the aspirant should learn about all of the paths of yoga and choose those elements which best suit his/her personality or practice them all in an integral, balanced way.

Enlightenment is the term used to describe the highest level of spiritual awakening. It means attaining such a level of spiritual awareness that one discovers the underlying unity of the entire universe as well as the fact that the source of all creation is the same source from which the innermost Self within every human heart arises. All forms of spiritual practice are directed toward the goal of assisting every individual to discover the true essence of the universe both externally, in physical creation, and internally, within the human heart, as the very root of human consciousness. Thus, many terms are used to describe the attainment of the goal of spiritual knowledge and the eradication of spiritual ignorance. Some of these terms are: *Enlightenment, Resurrection, Salvation, The Kingdom of Heaven, Moksha or Liberation, Buddha Consciousness, One With The Tao, Self-realization, to Know Thyself,* etc.

This book will focus on the Sema (Yoga) of Meditation as it was practiced in Ancient Egypt. When one thinks of the practice of meditation, usually the image comes to mind of India and Indian practitioners of Yoga or of Monks or Nuns. However, the practice of formal meditation goes way back to the pre-Christian era and even further, before yoga was developed in India. This booklet will present the essence of the first known formal meditation instructions which were given by the sages of Ancient Egypt. It is based on the hieroglyphic text that was found on the four walls of a small chamber which is entered from the "Hall of Columns" in the tomb of Seti I [Seti I] (second king of the 19th Dynasty), which is situated on the west bank of the Nile at the city of Waset (Thebes) in Egypt, Africa. The estimated date of completion of this temple was some time between 1306-1290 B.C.E. As with other myths of Ancient Egypt such as that of the Asarian Resurrection, the Myth of the "Destruction of Unrighteous Men and Women and the Story of Hetheru (Hathor) and Djehuty (Thoth)" was an ancient cultural myth dating to the inception of Ancient Egyptian civilization (5,000-3,000 B.C.E.) which did not originate with the construction of the Seti I tomb, but was only recorded there for posterity. As you will see, the **Ra Akhu Uaah (Glorious Light)** scripture has a close parallel in the earlier **Pert M Heru** text (Ancient Egyptian Book of Coming Forth By Day c.1800 B.C.E.) in reference to the "Divine Soul"-Chapter 85:

> *These are the words for making the transformation into the Soul of Tem. These words are to be said by Asar* _____ *who is Spiritually Victorious. "There is no going into the place of execution. I do not perish; I do not experience this. **I am Ra**, coming forth from Nun, the*

*Divine Soul, Creator of his own body parts. Unrighteousness is an abomination to me; I do not see it, for my thoughts are with Maat exclusively. I live in it! I am the God Hu[1], the one who does not perish in his name of "Divine Soul". I myself created my own name, with Nun. My name is Khepri and* **in the form of the god Ra I am All light**.

NOTE: This booklet is an expansion on the Glorious Light Meditation System first presented in the book *Meditation: The Ancient Egyptian Path to Enlightenment* by Muata Ashby. It is a detailed study of the philosophy and practice of that system of Meditation as it was practiced in Ancient Egypt.

**Figure 1: Image of the Sage King Seti I, Who commissioned the inscription of the *Ra Akhu Uaah* (Glorious Light Meditation teaching)**

---

[1] sense of taste, divine flavor.

**Figure 2: Seti I on a wall in the Temple of Asar in Abdu**

book of Exodus ordered the massacre of the Hebrew boys, in order to prevent a feared rebellion.[1] In 2006, Seti I was portrayed again in The Ten Commandments: The Musical.[1] <u>NONE of these depictions have a basis in history.</u>

Seti I was a Pharaoh in the New Kingdom Era of Ancient Egypt and father of Rameses the Great. In Popular Culture Seti I was portrayed in the 1956 film *The Ten Commandments*. Seti I was portrayed in the films *The Mummy* and its sequel *The Mummy Returns* as a pharaoh who is murdered by his high priest Imhotep and his mistress Ankh-s-n Amun. In the 1998 film *The Prince of Egypt* Seti (voiced by Patrick Stewart) is depicted as having been the Pharaoh who in the Biblical

13

**Figure 3: Seti I welcomed by the goddess Hetheru**

Seti I welcomed by the goddess Hetheru (Hathor). Painted relief from KV 17, the Tomb of Seti I in the Valley of the Kings. Limestone and pigment: height 2.26 m, width 1.05 m. Musée du Louvre Département des Antiquités égyptiennes E7.

**On the following page:**

**Figure 4: Tomb of Seti I, c. 1400 B.C.E. Above center pillar- Seti faces Asar in the Duat (Netherworld).**

**Figure 5: Story of Hetheru and Djehuty-Seti I tomb lines 1-21 of text**

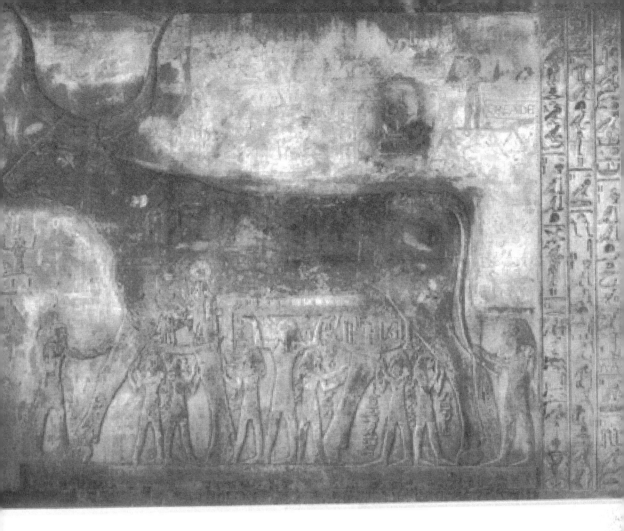

**Figure 6: Story of Hetheru and Djehuty-Seti I tomb lines 51-55 of text**

The Sacred Cow of Ancient Egypt

**Figure 7: The Goddess Nut from Ancient Egypt (Tomb of Seti I), reverenced as the life giving Cow.**

The cow is revered by the religion of Ancient Egypt due to it's association with the goddess. The Ancient Egyptian Goddess Nut is sometimes depicted as a cow, sometimes as the vast black sky, and sometimes as both. In this aspect as mother Goddess, she gives birth to the gods and goddesses which preside over and sustain Creation, as well as Creation itself. In her capacity as the cow she is an aspect of the cow goddess Mehurt, who represents the "fullness" aspect of the Primeval Ocean of Creation. Many of the Ancient Kamitan goddesses are often depicted with headdresses in the form of cow horns. The horns on the goddesses headdress, especially Aset (Isis) and Hetheru (Hathor), Nut and Mehurt, are a symbolic reference to the bovine (life-giving) nature of the female aspect of the Spirit. In Ancient Egypt goddess Nut was also known as the "Great Cow who gave birth to the sun," i.e. to the Creation and to the Divinity who presides over it.

**Figure 8: Below-the God Bes**

On the Following page:

THE MYTH OF HETHERU AND DJEHUTY IS ALSO RECOUNTED IN THE CHAPEL OF HETHERU AT THE ASET TEMPLE COMPLEX IN ASWAN EGYPT. THE PICTURE BELOW SHOWS PART OF THAT INSCRIPTION.

**Figure 9: Section of the Hetheru CHapel at the Aset Temple complex in Aswan Egypt**

## WHAT IS MEDITATION?

Meditation may be thought of or defined as the practice of mental exercises and disciplines to enable the aspirant to achieve control over the mind, specifically, to stop the vibrations of the mind due to unwanted thoughts, imaginations, etc. Just as the sun is revealed when the clouds disperse, so the light of the Self is revealed when the mind is free of thoughts, imaginations, ideas, delusions, gross emotions, sentimental attachments, etc. The Self, your true identity, is visible to the conscious mind.

The mind and nervous system are instruments of the Self, which it uses to have experiences in the realm of time and space, which it has created in much the same way as a person falls asleep and develops an entire dream world out of his/her own consciousness. It is at the unconscious and subconscious levels where the most intensive work of yoga takes place because it is here that the conscious identification of a person creates impressions in the mind and where desires based on those impressions develop. It is these desires that keep the aspirant involved in the realm of time and space or frees the aspirant from the world of time and space if they are sublimated into the spiritual desire for enlightenment. The desire to attain enlightenment is not viewed in the same manner as ego based desires; it is viewed as being aspiration which is a positive movement.

Externalized consciousness - distracted by egoism and worldly objects. ◁ ◁ ◁ ⌀

The light of the Self (consciousness) shines through the mind and this is what sustains life. The flow of consciousness in most people is from within moving outward. This causes them to be externalized and distracted and lose energy. Where the mind goes, energy flows. Have you ever noticed that you can "feel" someone looking at you? This is because there is a subtle energy being transmitted through their vision (which is an extension of the mind). Those who live in this externalized state of mind are not aware of the source of consciousness. Meditation as well as the other disciplines of yoga serve to reverse the flow of consciousness on itself so that the mind acts as a mirror which reveals the true Self.

Internalized consciousness of a yoga practitioner. ▷ ▷ ▷ ⌀

Most people are unaware that there are deeper levels to their being just as they are unaware of the fact that physical reality is not "physical." Quantum physics experiments have proven that the physical world is not composed of matter but of energy. This supports the findings of the ancient Sages who have taught for thousands of years that the reality which is experienced by the human senses is not an "Absolute" reality but a conditional one. Therefore, you must strive to rise beyond your conditioned mind and senses in order to perceive reality as it truly is.

20

*"Learn to distinguish the real from the unreal."*
—Ancient Egyptian Proverb

Human beings are not just composed of a mind, senses and a physical body. Beyond the physical and mental there is a soul level. This is the realm of the Higher Self which all of the teachings of yoga and the various practices of meditation are directed toward discovering. This "hidden" aspect of ourselves which is beyond the thoughts is known as Amun, Asar or Amenta in the Ancient Egyptian system of spirituality and as Brahman, in Indian Vedanta philosophy.

When you are active and not practicing or experiencing the wisdom of yoga, you are distracted from the real you. This distraction which comes from the desires, cravings and endless motion of thoughts in the mind is the *veil* which blocks your perception of your deeper essence, Neter Neter. These distractions keep you involved with the mind, senses, and body that you have come to believe is the real you. When your body is motionless and you are thinking and feeling, you are mostly associated with your mind. At times when you are not thinking, such as in the dreamless sleep state, then you are associated with your Higher Self. However, this connection in the dreamless sleep state is veiled by ignorance because you are asleep and not aware of the experience. In order to discover this realm you must consciously turn away from the phenomenal world which is distracting you from your inner reality. The practice of yoga accomplishes this task. Meditation, when backed up by the other disciplines of yoga, is the most powerful agent of self discovery. The practice of meditation allows one to create a higher awareness which affects all aspects of one's life, but most importantly, it gives the aspirant experiential knowledge of his/his true Self.

Universal Soul

_____

↙ ↓ ↘

Mind and Senses
(Astral Body and Astral World - the Duat or Netherworld)

_____

↙ ↓ ↘

Physical Body and Physical World

*What is the Goal of Meditation?*

Meditation may be thought of or defined as the practice of mental exercises and disciplines to enable the meditator to achieve control over the mind, specifically, to stop the vibrations of the mind due to unwanted thoughts, imaginations, etc.

Consciousness refers to the awareness of being alive and of having an identity. It is this characteristic which separates humans from the animal kingdom. Animals cannot become aware of their own existence and ponder the questions such as *Who am I?*, *Where am I going in life?*, *Where do I come from?*, etc. They cannot write books on history and create elaborate systems of social history based on ancestry, etc. Consciousness expresses itself in three modes. These are: Waking, Dream-Sleep and Dreamless-Deep-Sleep. However, ordinary human life is only partially conscious. When you are driving or walking, you sometimes lose track of the present moment. All of a sudden you arrive at your destination without having conscious awareness of the road which you have just traveled. Your mind went into an "automatic" mode of consciousness. This automatic mode of consciousness represents a temporary withdrawal from the waking world. This state is similar to a day dream (a dreamlike musing or fantasy). This form of existence is what most people consider as "normal" everyday waking consciousness. It is what people consider to be the extent of the human capacity to experience or be conscious.

The "normal" state of human consciousness cannot be considered as "whole" or complete because if it was there would be no experience of lapses or gaps in consciousness. In other words, every instant of consciousness would be accounted for. There would be no trance-like states wherein one loses track of time or awareness of one's own activities, even as they are being performed. In the times of trance or lapse, full awareness or consciousness is not present, otherwise it would be impossible to not be aware of the passage of time while engaged in various activities. Trance here should be differentiated from the religious or mystical form of trance like state induced through meditation. As used above, it refers to the condition of being so lost in solitary thought as to be unaware of one's surroundings. It may further be characterized as a stunned or bewildered condition, a fog, stupor, befuddlement, daze, muddled state of mind. Most everyone has experienced this condition at some point or another. What most people consider to be the "awake" state of mind in which life is lived is in reality only a fraction of the total potential consciousness which a human being can experience.

The state of automatic consciousness is characterized by mental distraction, restlessness and extroversion. The automatic state of mind exists due to emotions such as desire, anger and hatred which engender desires in the mind, which in turn cause more movement, distractions, delusions and lapses or "gaps" in human consciousness. In this condition, it does not matter how many desires are fulfilled. The mind will always be distracted and agitated and will never discover peace and contentment. If the mind were under control, meaning, if you were to remain fully aware and conscious of every feeling, thought and emotion in your mind at any given time, it would be impossible for you to be swayed or deluded by your thoughts into a state of relative unconsciousness or un-awareness. Therefore, it is said that those who do not have their minds under control are not fully awake and conscious human beings.

22

Meditation and Yoga Philosophy are disciplines which are directed toward increasing awareness. Awareness or consciousness can only be increased when the mind is in a state of peace and harmony. Thus, the disciplines of Meditation (which are part of the Yoga) are the primary means of controlling the mind and allowing the individual to mature psychologically and spiritually.

Psychological growth is promoted because when the mind is brought under control, the intellect becomes clear and psychological complexes such as anxiety and other delusions which have an effect even in ordinary people can be cleared up. Control of the mind and the promotion of internal harmony allows the meditator to integrate their personality and to resolve the hidden issues of the present, of childhood and of past lives.

When the mind has been brought under control, the expansion in consciousness leads to the discovery that one's own individual consciousness is not the total experience of consciousness. Through the correct practice of meditation, the individual's consciousness-awareness expands to the point wherein there is a discovery that one is more than just an individual. The state of "automatic consciousness" becomes reduced in favor of the experiences of increasing levels of continuous awareness. In other words, there is a decrease in daydreaming as well as the episodes of carrying out activities and forgetting oneself in them until they are finished (driving for example). Also, there is a reduced level of loss of awareness of self during the dreaming-sleep and dreamless-sleep states. Normally, most people at a lower level of consciousness-awareness become caught in a swoon or feinting effect which occurs at the time when one "falls" asleep or when there is no awareness of dreams while in the deep sleep state (dreamless-sleep). This swooning effect causes an ordinary person to lose consciousness of their own "waking state" identity and to assume the identity of their "dream subject" and thus, to feel that the dream subject as well as the dream world are realities in themselves.

This shift in identification from the waking personality to the dream personality to the absence of either personality in the dreamless-sleep state led ancient philosophers to discover that these states are not absolute realities. Philosophically, anything that is not continuous and abiding cannot be considered as real. Only what exists and does not change in all periods of time can be considered as "real." Nothing in the world of human experience qualifies as real according to this test. Nature, the human body, everything has a beginning and an end. Therefore, they are not absolutely real. They appear to be real because of the limited mind and senses along with the belief in the mind that they are real. In other words, people believe that matter and physical objects are real even though modern physics has proven that all matter is not "physical" or "stable." It changes constantly and its constituent parts are in reality composed of "empty spaces." Think about it. When you fall asleep, you "believe" that the dream world is "real" but upon waking up you believe it was not real. At the same time, when you fall asleep, you forget the waking world, your relatives and life history, and assume an entirely new history, relatives, situations and world systems. Therefore, philosophically, the ordinary states of consciousness which a human being experiences are limited and illusory. The waking, dream and dreamless-sleep states are only transient expressions of the deeper underlying consciousness. This underlying consciousness which witnesses the other three states is what Carl Jung referred to as the "Collective Unconscious." In Indian Philosophy this "fourth" state of consciousness-awareness is known as *Turia*. It is also referred to as "God Consciousness" or "Cosmic Consciousness."

The theory of meditation is that when the mind and senses are controlled and transcended, the awareness of the transcendental state of consciousness becomes evident. From here, consciousness-awareness expands, allowing the meditator to discover the latent abilities of the unconscious mind. When this occurs, an immense feeling of joy emerges from within, the desire for happiness and fulfillment through external objects and situations dwindles and a peaceful, transcendental state of mind develops. Also, the inner resources are discovered which will allow the practitioner to meet the challenges of life (disappointments, disease, death, etc.) while maintaining a poised state of mind.

When the heights of meditative experience are reached, there is a more continuous form of awareness which develops. It is not *lost* at the time of falling asleep. At this stage there is a discovery that just as the dream state is discovered to be "unreal" upon "waking up" in the morning, the waking state is also discovered to be a kind of dream which is transcended at the time of "falling asleep." There is a form of "continuous awareness" which develops in the mind which spans all three states of consciousness and becomes a "witness" to them instead of a subject bound by them.

Further, there is a discovery that there is a boundless source from which one has originated and to which one is inexorably linked. This discovery brings immense peace and joy wherein the worldly desires vanish in the mind and there is absolute contentment in the heart. This level of experience is what the Buddhists call *Mindfulness.* However, the history of mindfulness meditation goes back to the time of ancient India and Ancient Egypt. In India, the higher level of consciousness wherein automatic consciousness is eradicated and there is continuous awareness is called *Sakshin Buddhi.* From Vedanta and Yoga Philosophy, the teaching of the "witnessing consciousness" found even greater expression and practice in Buddhist philosophy and Buddhist meditation. Buddhi or higher intellect is the source of the word *Buddha,* meaning one who has attained wakefulness at the level of their higher intellect.

# What are Shetaut Neter and Sema Tawi? Where Were they Practiced and When?

## Where Was the Glorious Light Meditation and Shetaut Neter Practiced in Ancient Times?

The Glorious Light Meditation Practice was created and developed in Ancient Egypt by the Ancient Egyptians. Ancient Egyptian meditation is part of a larger spiritual practice called Shetaut Neter, the Ancient Egyptian religion. In ancient times Neterianism {Ancient Egyptian Religion) , was practice in the land of Kamit {Ancient Egypt) and the land of Kush. Kamit is located in the Northeastern corner of Africa. A civilization began to appear along the Nile River more than 12,000 years ago; this civilization became the Kamitan society. The Kamitans themselves say that they came from the south, from the land of Kush, originally as colonists. The following hieroglyphs are the original names of Ancient Egypt.

Qamit - Ancient Egypt

Qamit - blackness – black

Qamit - literature of Ancient Egypt – scriptures

Qamiu or variant                    Ancient Egyptians-people

of the black land.

# When Was Shetaut Neter and the Glorious Light Practiced?

Table 1: Timeline of Recorded Meditation Practice around the world

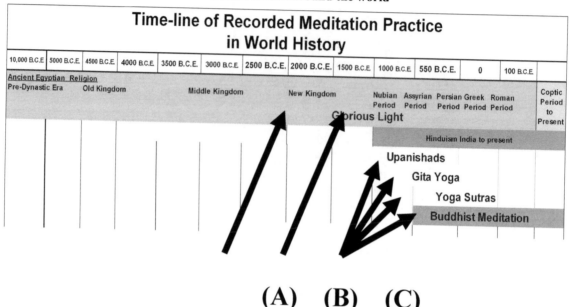

## (A) (B) (C)

**The Glorious Light Meditation was recorded in the Tomb of Seti I, c. 1400 B.C.E.**

While it is possible that formal meditation was practiced in other countries around the world earlier than the date of the G.L.M if it was it was not recorded for history. In this sense, the G.L.M is the erliest known recorded and fully documented "FORMAL" meditation system in human history.

(A) The G.L.M. is based on an Ancient Egyptian myth that stretches back into the Ancient Egyptian history. As with other myths of Ancient Egypt such as that of the Asarian Resurrection, the Myth of the "Destruction of Unrighteous Men and Women or the Story of Hetheru (Hathor) and Djehuty (Thoth)" was an ancient cultural myth dating to the inception of Ancient Egyptian civilization (5,000-3,000 B.C.E.) which did not originate with the construction of the Seti I temple, but was only recorded there for posterity.

(B) The **Ra Akhu Uaah (Glorious Light Meditation)** scripture has a close parallel in the earlier **Pert M Heru** text (Ancient Egyptian Book of Coming Forth By Day c.1800 B.C.E. {New Kingdom Era}) in reference to the "Divine Soul"-Chapter 85 of the **Pert M Heru** text.

(C) In history, the meditation systems of India and China come after the Glorious Light Meditation of Ancient Egypt.

# *Shetaut Neter and The Path of Awakening*

## WHAT IS SHETAUT NETER?

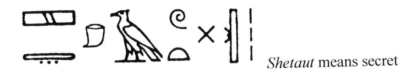 *Shetaut* means secret

*Neter* means Divinity.

"The teaching about the secret, hidden, Supreme Being"

Ancient Egyptian meditation practice is part of a larger system of spiritual practices called Shetaut Neter. Long ago, before any other civilization on earth arose, the Ancient Kamitian (Egyptian) Sages developed an extensive system of mythology and psychology as a means to assist human beings to develop to their full potential. This philosophy was called *Smai Taui* or *Smai Heru Set* (Egyptian Yoga). Who am I and what is this universe? These are questions which have perplexed humanity since the beginning of civilization. However, the Sages of ancient Africa were able to discover the secrets of the universe and of the innermost nature of the human heart. This discovery allowed them to create a civilization which lasted for tens of thousands of years and it enabled the creation of the magnificent monuments (Sphinx, Great Pyramids and Temples, which stand to this day. Also, Ancient Egyptian religion influenced and continues to influence the religions of Africa and other world religions of today such as Christianity, Hinduism and Islam. So what does this mean for us today? Many people have visited Egypt and have studied the work of Egyptologists but how many have been transformed into higher minded, more content, more powerful human beings who can rise to the challenges of life and aspire to achieve material and spiritual success? Many people have read about and studied Ancient Egyptian mythology but how is it possible to gain a deeper understanding of the mystical principles and how is it possible to integrate them into one's life so as to transform oneself into a higher being as the texts describe? How is it possible to go beyond the limited understanding of religion and the philosophy of modern culture which have not brought peace and prosperity to the world? In order to Succeed in Shetaut Neter one must also practice the Sema Tawi (Yoga) disciplines. When one practices the disciplines of Sema Tawi in Shetaut Neter this is called *Shedy* or *"Studies and practices to penetrate the mysteries."*

## Who is Neter?

# "Ntr"

Who is Ntr?

The symbol of Neter was described by an Ancient Kamitan sage as:

"That which is placed in the coffin"

The term Ntr, or Ntjr, come from the Ancient Egyptian hieroglyphic language which did not record its vowels. However, the term survives in the Coptic language as *"Nutar."* The same Coptic meaning (divine force or sustaining power) applies in the present as it did in ancient times, It is a symbol composed of a wooden staff that was wrapped with strips of fabric, like a mummy. The strips alternate in color with yellow, green and blue. The mummy in Kamitan spirituality is understood to be the dead but resurrected Divinity. So the Nutar is actually every human being who does not really die, but goes to live on in a different form. Further, the resurrected spirit of every human being is that same Divinity. Phonetically, the term Nutar is related to other terms having the same meaning, the latin "Natura," Spanish Naturalesa, English "Nature" and "Nutriment", etc. In a real sense, as we will see, Natur means power manifesting as Neteru and the Neteru are the objects of creation, i.e. "nature."

What is Shetaut Neter? The Ancient Egyptians were African peoples who lived in the north-eastern quadrant of the continent of Africa. They were descendants of the Nubians, who had themselves originated from farther south into the heart of Africa at the great lakes region, the sources of the Nile River. They created a vast civilization and culture earlier than any other society in known history and organized a nation which was based on the concepts of balance and order as well as spiritual enlightenment. These ancient African people called their land Kamit and soon after developing a well ordered society they began to realize that the world is full of wonders but life is fleeting and that there must be something more to human existence. They developed spiritual systems that were designed to allow human beings to understand the nature of this secret being who is the essence of all Creation. They called this spiritual system "Shtaut Ntr."

### THE SUPREME BEING IS ONE

"God is the father of beings. God is the eternal One... and infinite and endures forever. God is hidden and no man knows God's form. No man has been able to seek out God's likeness. God is hidden to Gods and men... God's name remains hidden... It is a mystery to his children, men, women and Gods. God's names are innumerable, manifold and no one knows their number... though God can be seen in form and observation of God can be made at God's appearance, God cannot be understood... God cannot be seen with mortal eyes... God is invisible and inscrutable to Gods as well as men."

-Portions from the Egyptian Book of Coming forth by Day and
the papyrus of Nesi-Khensu

The statements above give the understanding that God is the unfathomable mystery behind all phenomena, which cannot be discerned "even by the gods." However, God is the unfathomable mystery as well as the innermost essence of his children. This means that God is transcendental, the unmanifest, but also what is manifest as well. In order to perceive this reality it is necessary to transcend ordinary human vision. When this transcendental Self is spoken about through different names and metaphors, the idea often emerges that there are many faces to the ultimate divinity or Supreme Being. Nevertheless, as has been previously discussed, it must be clear that all the Neterian spiritual traditions are in reality referring to the same Supreme Being, the transcendental reality.

UA ⸂⸗◻𓀀 or "One,"
UA NETER ⸂⸗◻𓀀𓆈 or "One God,"
"Only One" ⸂⸗◻𓀀⸂⸗◻𓅆,
"Only One Without a second" ⸂⸗◻𓀀⸂⸗◻𓅆𓂓𓏤𓏭𓀁
"One One" ⸂⸗◻⸂⸗◻𓏭𓀀

The following passages come from the Egyptian Book of Coming Forth By Day (Chapter. clxxiii):

"I praise thee, Lord of the Gods, God One, living in truth."

The following passage is taken from a hymn where princess Nesi-Khensu glorifies Amen-Ra:

"August Soul which came into being in primeval time, the great god living in truth, the first Nine Gods who gave birth to the other two Nine Gods,[2] the being in whom every God existeth One One, ⸂⸗◻⸗◻𓏭𓀀 the creator of the kings who

---

[2] Ancient Egyptian mythology conceives of creation as an expression of God in which there are nine primordial cosmic principles or forces in the universe. These first nine may be seen as the cause from which all other qualities of nature *(the other two Nine Gods)* or creative forces in nature arise.

appeared when the earth took form in the beginning, whose birth is hidden, whose forms are manifold, whose germination cannot be known."

# The term "Neterianism"

is derived from the name "Shetaut Neter." What is Neterianism? The term "Neterianism" is derived from the term Shetaut Neter. Those who follow the spiritual path of Shetaut Neter are referred to as "Neterians." When referring to the religion of ancient Egypt, itself, the term Neterianism will be used. This term will be substituted for or will be used interchangeably with the term Ancient Egyptian Religion or Kamitan Religion or spirituality. All these are referring to the same thing: Neterianism, Shetaut Neter, Ancient Egyptian Religion, or Kamitan Religion.

Those who follow the spiritual path of Shetaut Neter are therefore referred to as "Neterians."

Neterianism is the science of Neter, that is, the study of the secret or mystery of Neter, the enigma of that which transcends ordinary consciousness but from which all creation arises. The world did not come from nothing, nor is it sustained by nothing. Rather it is a manifestation of that which is beyond time and space but which at the same time permeates and maintains the fundamental elements. In other words, it is the substratum of Creation and the essential nature of all that exists.

## ETYMOLOGY OF THE TERM SHETAUT NETER

Here we have the term *Shetaut* or *Sheta* meaning "hidden, difficult to understand, hard to get through, a mystery." The term *Shetaut Kepheru*, means hidden, creator of forms; *Shetitu* means: "writings related to the hidden teachings"; *Shet-Ta* means "the land covered by the Nile." When the Nile water is overflowing, the land is covered, so it means covered, or shrouded.

*Sheta* means "the secret hidden Divinity." *Shetaut Aset* means "the Divinity in the hidden abode or throne;" (Aset means abode or throne). *Shetai* means "hidden secret Being, The Divine essential nature." This is the etymology of the term Shetaut in Shetaut Neter.

## The Goal of Shetaut Neter: The Great Awakening

What is the purpose of Neterianism? What is the purpose of all the disciplines of Neterian spirituality?

The end of all the Neterian disciplines is to discover the meaning of "Who am I," to unravel the mysteries of life and to fathom the depths of eternity and infinity. This is the task of all human beings and it is to be accomplished in this very lifetime.

This can be done by learning the ways of the Neteru, emulating them and finally becoming like them, *Akhu*, (enlightened beings), walking the earth as giants and accomplishing great deeds such as the creation of the universe!

The Kemetic word "Nehast" means attaining that sublime and highest goal of life which is Spiritual Enlightenment, to experience the state of conscious awareness of oneness with the Divine and all Creation which transcends individuality born of ego consciousness...like the river uniting with the ocean, discovering the greater essential nature of Self... that state which bestows abiding blessedness, peace, bliss, contentment, fulfillment, freedom from all limitation and supreme empowerment.

## THE GREAT AWAKENING

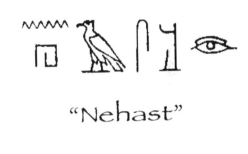

"Nehast"

The ultimate goal of life is *Nehast*. Nehast means "Spiritual Awakening." It is the spiritual awakening that leads one to discover the glory of life beyond death, discovering immortality, eternity and supreme peace. This is the coveted goal of all spiritual aspirants in all religions of the world, past or present. This is the goal that is to be striven for in life. It is the most worthy goal because all else will fade away one day. All else is perishable, fleeting and illusory. And this is what is called the Great Awakening, Nehast, the Awakening to spiritual consciousness. In the upper left hand corner of the slide you can see Asar Awakening from the tomb being assisted by the four sons of Heru. These four sons are also the first Shemsu, the Shemsu Heru. They are the ones who follow Asar, and they help to resurrect him. Nehast means to wake-up, to awaken to the higher existence.

The question is how to attain that lofty goal (Nehast). Just because all religions are striving for that does not mean they are engaging the correct methods to achieve that goal. They may have the dogma, the idea, but that does not mean that they have the how. One cannot attain resurrection, the spiritual awakening, just by faith. Faith must be followed by action, living in accordance with the teachings. That leads to growing understanding of and finally experience of the Divine. The end of all of the Neterian disciplines is to discover the meaning of "Who am I?," to unravel the mysteries of life, and to fathom the depths of eternity and infinity. This is the task of all human beings, and it is to be accomplished in this very lifetime. This can be done by learning the ways of the Neteru and emulating them, and finally becoming like them, *Akhu* walking the earth as giants and accomplishing great deeds.

*Akhu* is a term that we use in Neterian Theology that means "enlightened beings." *Akh* is a person who has achieved *Nehast*, who has achieved awakening...the great Enlightenment.

## THE FOLLOWER OF NETERIANISM

*"Shemsu Neter"*

"Follower (of) Neter"

The term "Neterianism" is derived from the name "Shetaut Neter." Those who follow the spiritual path of Shetaut Neter are therefore referred to as "Neterians."

Neterianism is the science of Neter, that is, the study of the secret or mystery of Neter, the enigma of that which transcends ordinary consciousness but from which all creation arises. The world did not come from nothing, nor is it sustained by nothing. Rather it is a manifestation of that which is beyond time and space but which at the same time permeates and maintains the fundamental elements. In other words, it is the substratum of Creation and the essential nature of all that exists.

So those who follow the Neter may be referred to as Neterians.

# What is the Origin of Shetaut Neter and Who Was the Founder of Neterianism?

One of the most important questions in life for followers of any religion is who started it? This is not important from an absolute point of view but it is important from a cultural, mythic and psychomythological point of view. In order to understand who founded Neterianism, the teaching of Shetaut Neter, we must also understand the origins of creation. In the sacred scriptures[3] of Shetaut Neter we are told that Creation is a cycle. That is, that Creation occurs cyclically. God brings creation into existence and then dissolves it again.

## LORD KHEPRI, FOUNDER OF NETERIANISM

According to High Priest Manetho, the current cycle of Creation began around the year 36,000 B.C.E. In the beginning there was nothing more than a watery mass, a primeval ocean, called Nun. Nun is the body of Khepri. Prior to the creation, Khepri remained in a recumbent posture. He rested on the back of the great serpent **Asha**-hrau ("many faces").

In the form of Ra Khepri arose from the primeval ocean (Nun) with his boat, accompanied by his company of Gods and Goddesses. Nun lifted the boat from the depths of the ocean so it could engender Creation and sail for millions of years..

---

[3] See the book *African Religion Vol. 1 Anunian Theology* by Muata Ashby

From that Nun the Divine Spirit arose by stimulating Asha-hrau to move and churn the ocean. Then he named himself Khepri, Creator. Khepri called out his own name and

⊗ ▱ **dchn** –vibrations were infused in the ocean and waves vere formed. Just as there are many waves in the ocean with many shapes and sizes, the objects of the world came into being in the form of elements, Ra (fire), Shu (air-space), Tefnut (water), Geb (earth), Nut (ether). Everything in creation emanates from the Nun or primordial ocean, and expresses in the form of elements in succeeding levels of denseness. These elements also manifest in the form of the opposites of Creation (man-woman, up-down, white-black) which appear to be exclusive and separate from each other, but which are in reality complements to each other.

## Khepri and the Creation Myth

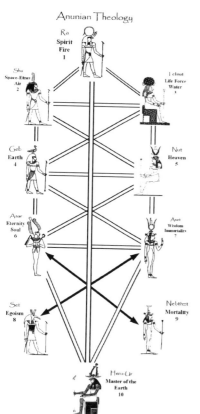

Khepri congealed the Nun, his own body, into all the forms of Creation. The first spot that was congealed from the Nun is called ⌡○⌡○⌡ **Benben,** the first place, the Ben-Ben dot, •, of Creation. That dot is the center point in the symbol of Khepr-Ra ⊙. That dot is the very point at the top of the Pyramid ▱△ *mr- Obelisk,* ∿⌡ *tekhnu.* The pyramid-obelisk symbolizes the mound that formed from that initial spot. Khepri sat atop the hill of Creation and all solid ground took form underneath him.

Khepri then bought forth Creation by emerging in a boat. The Nun waters lifted him and his boat up with his great arms. He brought nine divinities with him in that boat, lesser gods and goddesses, to help him sustain the

Creation and lead human beings on the righteous path to life and spiritual enlightenment.

**Figure 10: The Kemetic Tree of Gods and Goddesses of Anunian Theurgy and the Boat of Ra**

Having created Creation, Khepri now sails the ocean, which has now become Creation itself, with his divinities, on the divine boat. Khepri-Ra and the *pauti*, Company of gods and goddesses, travels in the Boat of Millions of Years, which traverses the heavens, and thereby sustains creation through the wake of the boat that sends ripples (vibrations) throughout the Nun, which has taken the form of Creation. The act of "Sailing" signifies the motion in creation. Motion implies that events occur in the realm of time and space relative to each other, thus, the phenomenal universe comes into existence as a mass of moving essence we call the elements. Prior to this motion, there was the primeval state of being without any form and without existence in time or space. The gods and goddesses of the boat form the court of Kheper-Ra. As Ra, the Supreme Being governed the earth for many thousands of years. He created the world, the planets, the stars and the galaxies; he also created animals, as well as men and women. During this time Ra instituted his son, Djehuty as his Minister but Ra ruled from his throne on earth. In the beginning, men and women revered the Divine, but after living for a very long time, they began to take Ra for granted. They became arrogant and vain. Ra sent his daughter, Hetheru, to punish them, but she forgot her way and became lost in the world. Then He left for his abode in heaven and gave the earthly throne to his son Shu, and daughter, Tefnut. After a long period of time, they turned over the throne to their children, Geb and Nut. After some time again, Geb and Nut gave the throne to their children, Asar and Aset, and so on in a line of succession throughout history, down to the Pharaohs of Kamit.

Lord Khepri manifests as Neberdjer, "All-encompassing Divinity." Aspirants are to say:

*tu-a m shems n Neberdjer*
*"I am a follower of Neberdjer*

*er sesh n Kheperu*
*in accordance with the writings of Lord Kheperu"*

So, the Shetaut Neter "Mystery teachings" were originally given by the Creator, Khepri. In this capacity he is known as *Shetaut Kheperu, "hidden Creator of forms."* Lord Djehuty codified these Mystery teachings into the hieroglyphic texts, and

35

these teachings were passed down to succeeding generations of divinities, sages and priests and priestesses throughout history.

So Lord Khepri (Ra) imparted his *Sebait,* wisdom and philosophy of spiritual existence, the Shetaut Neter, to the gods and goddesses and especially to his son Djehuty. Thus, Lord Khepri, the Self Created Divinity, is the founder of Shetaut Neter. The codifier. The one who wrote down the teaching of Khepri, was his first main disciple, Djehuty. Djehuty has the body of a man and the head of an Ibis bird. He also has another form as a baboon. The teaching that Lord Khepri gave to Djehuty became known as *Shetitu*, the hidden teaching, and it was conveyed through the *Medtu Neteru* (hieroglyphic texts).

The teachings of the Shetaut Neter were espoused through the spiritual traditions of Ancient Egypt, which were related to varied gods and goddesses.

# "Medtu Neteru"

The teachings of the Neterian Traditions are conveyed in the scriptures of the Neterian Traditions. The Medu Neter was used through all periods by priests and priestesses – mostly in monumental inscriptions such as the Pyramid texts, Obelisks, temple inscriptions, etc. – since Pre-Dynastic times. It is the earliest form of writing in known history. Thus, these Shetaut (mysteries- rituals, wisdom, philosophy) about the Neter (Supreme Being) are related in the writings of the hidden teaching. And those writings are referred to as *Medu Neter* or "Divine Speech," the writings of the god Djehuty (Ancient Egyptian god of the divine word). *Medu Neter* also generally refers to any Kamitan hieroglyphic texts or inscriptions. The term Medu Neter makes use of a special hieroglyph, which means "*medu*" or "staff - walking stick-speech." This means that speech is the support for the Divine, . Thus, just as the staff supports an elderly person, the hieroglyphic writing (the word) is a prop or support (staff) which sustains the Divine in the realm of time and space. That is, these Divine writings (*Medu Neter*) contain the wisdom which enlightens us about the Divine, *Shetaut Neter.* If *Shetitu* is mastered through the study of the Medu Neter then the spiritual aspirant becomes ⟨hieroglyphs⟩ Maakheru or true of thought, word and deed, that is, purified in body, mind and soul. The symbol medu is static while the symbol of Kheru is dynamic.

The term Maakheru uses the glyph ⟨hieroglyph⟩ *kheru*, which is a rudder – oar (rowing), and a symbol of voice, meaning that purification occurs through the righteous movement of the word, when it is used (rowing-movement) to promote Maat (virtue, order, peace, harmony and truth). So Medu Neter is the potential word and Maa kheru is the perfected word.

The hieroglyphic texts (Medu Neter) become useful (Maakheru) in the process of religion when they are used as ⟨hieroglyphs⟩ *hekau* - the Ancient Egyptian "Words of Power." They are to be ⟨hieroglyphs⟩ *Hesi*, chanted and ⟨hieroglyphs⟩ *Shmai*- sung, and thereby one performs ⟨hieroglyphs⟩ *Dua* or adoration of the Divine. The divine word allows the speaker to control the gods and goddesses, who actually are the cosmic forces in Creation. Human beings are a higher order beings, and they can attain this higher state of consciousness if they learn about the nature of the universe and elevate themselves through virtue and wisdom.

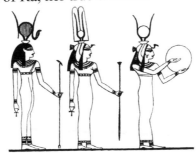

Above: Lord Djehuty imparted the teaching he learned from Khepri to goddess Hetheru (here in the form of a cow goddess). She became lost in the world and forgot her true identity. He showed her how to discover her true Self, how to know herself and how to find her way back to heaven, to her father Ra. Here Djehuty is shown presenting to Hetheru, the healed right eye of Ra, her true essence.

**Above: Goddess Hetheru as Queen**

Lord Khep-Ra knew that human beings needed guidance, so he sent his great grandchildren, Asar and Aset, to be teachers and role models for human beings on earth. Lord Djehuty also imparted the hidden knowledge of life to Aset and Asar, so that they would lead people on earth in a righteous manner, showing them the path of peace, prosperity and spiritual enlightenment. Asar and Aset established the Shetaut Neter, "Divine Mysteries," ritual worship and Ancient Egyptian religion. When human beings become too involved in the world they forget their true nature, and so the Temple,

*Het Neter* {House of the Divinity {God(dess)}-Temple}, was created, where the pressure of the world can be relieved, and an association with something other than the worldly perspective (i.e., with Divinity) can occur.

Such a place and its teaching are needed so that the mind can become aware of higher possibilities and turn away from *umt-ab-* "mental dullness" due to *Khemn,* "ignorance," and be led to *Nehast* –"Resurrection, spiritual awakening," *Akhu,* "enlightenmened people" and so that human beings may become *Sheps-* "nobility, honor, venerable-ness, honored ancestors."

Above: *Aset nurses baby Heru*

As we learn in the teaching of the Asarian Resurrection, Aset learned the Mystery teachings from Lord Djehuty. Aset is the ancient African prototype of the mother and child which is popular all over Africa, and also in Christian and Indian iconography with the birth of Jesus and Krishna, respectively. The mother is the first teacher. Aset not only raised Heru, but also initiated him into the mysteries of life and creation, with the teaching she learned from Djehuty and Khepri, in order to enlighten him and make him strong for the battle of life.

Heru is the redeemer, the challenger, the one who stands up for his father, Asar, and liberates him from the imprisonment of death. Heru represents spiritual aspiration and success in the spiritual path. Heru reestablishes order after defeating the evil Set, and takes the throne of Kamit. In his form as Heru Behdet, Heru is a warrior (above). He

fights for truth, justice and freedom for all. Heru, the redeemer, the warrior, the greatest advocate of Asar (the soul) and triumphant aspirant is the one who leads the aspirant to the initiation hall. As seen here (at left), Heru is often the one shown leading the aspirant by the hand, into the inner shrine. In rituals, the priest wears a Heru mask in the context of a ritual theatrical ceremony of the temple that is meant to awaken the glory of the Neterian teaching in the heart of the aspirant.

What is the purpose of life? In order to tread a true and beneficial path in life it is necessary to understand what is good in life and is worth pursuing, as opposed to what is not true or worth pursuing. The philosophy provides insight. The wisdom teachings related to this important issue need to be carefully studied and diligently reflected upon until the message is understood clearly by your mind.

Kamitan Proverbs:

"The purpose of human life is to achieve a state of consciousness apart from bodily concerns"

"Men and women are to become godlike through a life of virtue and cultivation of the spirit through scientific knowledge, practice, and bodily discipline."

"Salvation is freeing of the soul from the bodily fetters. Becoming a god through knowledge and wisdom, controlling the forces of the cosmos instead of being a slave to them. Subduing the lower nature and through awakening the higher Self, ending the cycle of rebirth and dwelling with the neters who direct and control the great plan."

What should be the purpose of life? Should the purpose of life be to get rich, to have lots of fame, or a big family? No, the purpose is to become God-like, and further, to become one with God!

Now, if you decide to adopt Shetaut Neter, and you meet, say, a Christian person on the road, how will you respond to them? Perhaps you have friends in your family who are Christians, Muslims, etc., and they may ask you what are you doing? You may answer: "I am practicing African Religion." "I am practicing Neterianism." Suppose they now ask you, "What is your goal in Neterianism?" Do not tell them you are trying to become a god or a goddess. Don't waste your time getting into that kind of conflict, because in their view only Jesus can do that. But in African Religion… everybody can do that, and not in some future time, but right now…in your lifetime.

In ancient times, there was a certain genre of literature called "The Harper's Songs." This is a special genre of ancient Egyptian literature that deals with the understanding of the meaning and purpose of life. Through the following Harper's Song, the purpose of life becomes clear. The song goes:

"I have heard these songs, which are in the ancient tombs
Which tell of the virtues of life on earth, and make little of life in the Neterkert (cemetery).
Why then do likewise to eternity?
It is a place of justice, without fear,
where an uproar is forbidden,
where no one attacks his fellow.
This place has no enemies;
All our relatives have lived in it from time immemorial.
and with millions more to come.
I joined in?
It is not possible to linger in Egypt
No one can escape from going west (note: west is the land to death, the land of the afterlife, the Netherworld)
One's acts on earth are like a dream
Welcome safe and sound,
to whoever arises in the West"

The Harper is telling us we cannot linger on earth. We must plan for our departure, and that our acts on earth here are like a dream. If you consider what the Harper's Song is saying, it is like when you have a dream when you are asleep. Your dream appears to be very real, but when you wake up from it in the morning, then you realize that it is not real. What happens when you go to sleep? When you go to sleep you believe that dream world is real, and this waking world is unreal. Which is the reality then? Do you see the high philosophy that is going on here? It means that there is something within you that is beyond the changing realms of consciousness… the waking and the dream state.

How are you to discover that state that is beyond illusion? How are you to elevate yourself to transcend this mortal finite existence? Accomplishing this is what is referred to as becoming gods and goddesses. The question then becomes how is this to be achieved? It is wonderful for me to tell you what Shetaut Neter is all about. But it is also important that you know how this is achieved. I am sure that you have heard of that saying "many are called and few are chosen."

Those of you who are studying this now, as opposed to the millions of people who are out there in the world – you are reading this because you are ready to pursue some new path to life. You are ready to discover some insight that leads you to the answers to your questions, and most likely, as to the true purpose in life and the source of pain in life. I am mainly just confirming what you already know anyway, because you have the wisdom inside you, but you have to know how to tap into it.

# What is Sema Tawi
## "Sema Tawi or Smai Tawi"
### (From Chapter 4 of the *Prt m Hru*)

In Chapter 4 and Chapter 17 of the *Prt m Hru,* a term "*Sma (Sema* or *Smai)* Tawi" is used. It means "Union of the two lands of Egypt," ergo "Egyptian Yoga." The two lands refer to the two main districts of the country (North and South). In ancient times, Egypt was divided into two sections or land areas. These were known as Lower and Upper Egypt. In Ancient Egyptian mystical philosophy, the land of Upper Egypt relates to the divinity Heru (Horus), who represents the Higher Self, and the land of Lower Egypt relates to Set, the divinity of the lower self. So *Sema (Smai) Tawi* means "the union of the two lands" or the "Union of the lower self with the Higher Self. The lower self relates to that which is negative and uncontrolled in the human mind including worldliness, egoism, ignorance, etc. (Set), while the Higher Self relates to that which is above temptations and is good in the human heart as well as in touch with Transcendental consciousness (Heru). Thus, we also have the Ancient Egyptian term *Sema (Smai) Heru-Set,* or the union of Heru and Set. So Sema (Smai) Tawi or Sema (Smai) Heru-Set are the Ancient Egyptian words which are to be translated as "Egyptian Yoga."

 "Shedy"

## WHAT IS SHEDY?

Shedy means: "to penetrate the mysteries", "to study the teachings deeply and gain insight into their meaning." What Are The Disciplines of Shedy:

There were 4 aspects of Shedy (Spiritual Practice):
Sedjm - "Listening"
Maat - "Right Actions"
Uash - "Devotion to God"
Uaa - "Meditation"

For those who have chosen Shetaut Neter as their path, it is necessary to enter into a process called Shedy. Shedy means. Each discipline of Shedy is designed to inform, purify, elevate and establish the Shemsu on the path to awakening. These are the steps to the effective practice of religion that will lead a human being to maturity and spiritual realization. In order to be effective the disciplines must be listened to, acted upon and meditated upon under the correct guidance.

1-Listen to the teaching: **"Mestchert"** "Listening, to fill the ears, listen attentively"

2- Study, reflection on the teaching: **MAZIT** "to think, to ponder, to fix attention, concentration" and right actions based on the teachings: Learn the path of Virtue, that is **Maat** . Even in your present circumstance learn to develop divine values, be righteous, treat others righteously and fairly, uphold truth and justice for all. This will purify you and will allow you to experience the benefits of steps 1-3 above. This is your duty. Uphold your responsibilities. Be a virtuous and you will discover inner peace and higher consciousness and you will also affect those around you. So it is very important to practice the teachings to the highest possible degree. Acquire the books that relate the teaching. If possible get audio taped lectures from qualified preceptors, that explain the teaching. Then your efforts will be most effective in transforming your life and discovering true redemption and divine glory.

3-Then Meditate upon the teaching: **uaa** "Meditation"

# PART I: The Psychomythology of the Glorious Light Teaching

## *The Creation of the Universe, The Destruction of Unrighteous Men and Women / The Story of Hetheru and Djehuty*

The story of Hetheru and Djehuty is told through an Ancient Egyptian *Matnu* or Myth. A myth is a kind of language that is not necessarily literally or historically true but conveys true wisdom teachings about the nature of human and spiritual origins, the meaning of life and the path to discover the answers to the important questions of life. As with other African traditions, the Ancient Egyptian spiritual tradition enjoins that a mythic teaching or *maut*. When a teaching is given there are three components necessary in order for it to be viable and effective. There are three stages or levels of religion, the

Mythic: *Matnu* 𓂀𓏤𓏠𓏜𓆑𓏏 - legend, story. Ritual: *Aru* 𓁹𓂋𓏤𓅃 - ritual – ceremony. And the *Shetaut Neter* 𓈖𓏏𓂋𓐍𓏏𓏥 -Mystical. The myth is given through *Sdjedt* 𓋴𓆓𓂧𓏤 - story telling – to speak proverbs – speak tales. In the myth stage the *Shemsu.* 𓌞𓋴𓅱, followers of a religion learn the story. Again, the story is not necessarily historical although it may have historical elements embedded in it, such as names of places or objects or people that really did exist. Yet, human beings alive today are not different from those who lived thousands of years ago in the sense of their perceptions and capacity to evolve spiritually and their desires. They have the same desires, the same concerns and the same yearning to discover and experience immortality and transcendental consciousness. Thus, if a myth is constructed correctly it can remain relevant in perpetuity as it relates to universal principles that will affect all human beings throughout all time periods. Myth is a special language that relates to the higher aspect of spirit in all things. Therefore, the myth is primarily, though not exclusively, metaphorical, relating to truths that cannot often be expressed in physical terms and yet use physical terminology, similes and parables to point the mind in the direction of the transcendent. Thus, myth uses the phenomenological language of the mind because the mind is limited and gross even though it is referring to what is spiritual and transcendental. The *maut* 𓃀𓏠𓂻𓏜 is the moral of the myth or story that is to be remembered. It is the important teaching imparted through the myth that is impressed on the mind.

43

# Background to the Myth

In Kemetic philosophy, mythology holds the key to the essential teachings of the mind and its various states and functions as well as the means to overcome it. Therefore, in order to understand the teachings related to meditation it is necessary to understand the psychomythology of the mind. What follows is an overview of the myth of Hetheru and Djehuty, wherein the Glorious Light Meditation Scriptrue is contained. In the scripture, it's writer, Lord Djehuty, instructs that before the meditation is practiced the story should be read, in other words, known, remembered, recited, commemorated, etc. Then the practice of the actual meditation may proceed.

**Figure 11: The Goddess Hetheru and the God Djehuty**

Above: Left-The goddess Hetheru in the form of a woman.
Right– The god Djehuty in his two principal forms.

## *The Image of Ra and its mystical symbolism*

Ra is the sun. His primary symbol is the sundisk, which is the means by which his lifeforce and destructive power manifests. He has a name which cannot be spoken and that name represents the power that sustains his form in time and space as well as Creation itself. The sun is the symbol of the Divine Self par excellence because it shines continuously. It does not have light and dark as the earth. It is constantly full light. Thus, it transcends time and space. Likewise, the Divine Self transcends changes in consciousness, it is absolute, unlike human beings, who change constantly, from waking to dream and then sleep, from death to life and then to death, youth to old age, i.e. the changes of the opposites. In the Divine Self there are no opposites, only the singular transcendental essence. Hetheru represents the projection of that essence into time and space. In this capacity she symbolizes all human beings, who are sparks of divine consciousness. When that projection occurs, there is a form of delusion that occurs wherein the ray of light forgets whence it came from. Then it needs to be led back to the knowledge of the Self, the Divine Light. This is the central teaching of the Myth of Hetheru and Djehuty.

**Figure 12: The God Ra and the Sundisk**

45

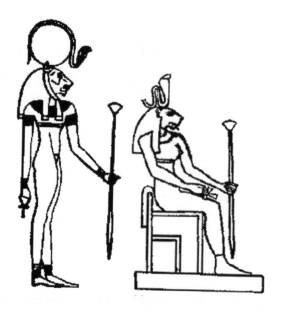

**Figure 13: The Goddesses Sekhemit and Tefnut**

Above left: Hetheru in her feline aspect as Sekhmit, the lioness goddess.

Sekhmit is the goddess who presides over Sekhem or the Serpent Power Life Force of all things.

Above right: The goddess Tefnut. Tefnut symbolizes the potential dynamic energy, the Life Force within all creation. She is that which allows creation to have movement. She is represented as a lioness and she is related to the Ancient Egyptian goddess known as Sekhmit.

Hetheru is an archetype for all goddesses. In Anunian Theurgy[4] Tefnut is the leonine power of goddess energy and thus she is an aspect of Hetheru in the form of Sekhemit. Hetheru is at the same time the fire spitting serpent that encircles the sundisk, which emits lifeforce, *Sekhem,* and can sustain life or destroy life. So she herself is that power of the sundisk, which is the same means used by Goddess Sekhemit to destroy the unrighteous in favor of what is good, true and devoted to Ra.

---

[4] See the books *Anunian Theology* and *The Kemetic Tree of Life* by Muata Ashby

46

# *Ra, Djehuty and Hetheru*

**Figure 14: The Goddess Hetheru and the God Djehuty**

This is the story of Hetheru (Hetheru) and Djehuty which was written in Ancient Egypt thousands of years ago. It was told on temple inscriptions. Hetheru is the goddess of beauty and passion. She has many forms. At times she is a beautiful woman, at other times she is a cow, and still at other times she is the Eye of Ra, the very scorching power of the sun itself.

Ra is the Creator of the universe. He is the very source of all that exists. The *Pautti* or *Psedjet* (Ennead or nine divinities), the primordial gods and goddesses of Creation, emanated from the Supreme Being. Ra or Ra-Tem arose out of the *"Nu,"* the Primeval waters, the hidden essence, and began sailing the *"Boat of Millions of Years"* which included the "neteru." The neteru of the Pautti are Ra-Atum, Shu, Tefnut, Geb, Nut, Asar (Osiris), Aset (Isis), Set, and Nebthet. Hetheru, Djehuty and Maat came into existence at the instant of Creation.

**Dua Ra, Dua Ra, Dua Ra Khepra**

**Figure 15-***Above: Ra as the midday sun (left) and as the setting sun.*

Ra created human beings and he ruled the earth for thousands of years. A time came when human beings began to feel arrogant and egoistic. They began to think that Ra was old and weak and that he was not the creator, but that they sustain themselves without any divine agency. They began to blaspheme and ridicule him. This was reported to Ra by his ministers and courtiers, the neteru (gods and goddesses of the creation). Ra decided to punish the unrighteous human beings by letting loose upon them his daughter, Hetheru, who would be the instrument of his judgement upon them.

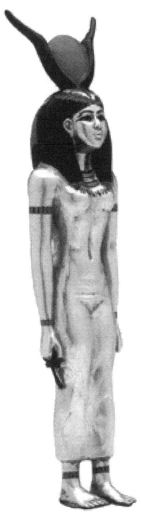

Hetheru agreed to become the instrument of punishment against the evil men and women that were acting unrighteously, blaspheming Ra and turning away from his glorious nature. Hetheru is Ra's power that he can project, for she is actually the serpent in his sundisk, a fire-spitting serpent, whose venum are the sunrays. Just as sunrays can burn and scorch the earth, her rays can destroy evil and unrighteousness. The power of her radiance and heat can burn up that which is wrong, iniquitous or unjust or unvirtuous. Here we must remember that we can say that she destroys evil but evil should be understood as the unrighteousness that arises out of egoistic desires, so she can destroy the productions of egoism and egoism itself. So the propitiation of Hetheru is a serious effort to cleanse the personality, thus when she is called upon in the form she will turn into she must be properly attended to and respected, otherwise that same power can lose control and destroy all..

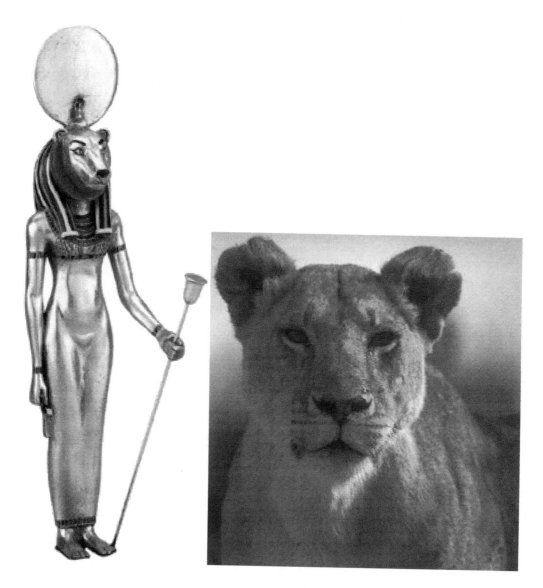

**Figure 16: The goddess Sekhemit**

Hetheru transformed herself into the form of a lioness. She began to kill the unrighteous people and then liked it so much that she began to kill indiscriminately. She left Egypt in search of more prey and the neteru wondered if she would ever stop or if she would kill everyone, including the gods and goddesses as well. When she left Egypt the people were devastated. Gloom filled the atmosphere. Everything was in decline. The forces of darkness, chaos, injustice, unrighteousness and evil began to take control of the land because Hetheru, who was the power of Ra which he used to uphold righteousness and truth, had left the land. Ra, the Supreme Being, creator of the gods and goddesses and the entire universe, became sorrowful at the loss of his daughter, his very power. Hetheru took pleasure in her new form. She killed the evil man and women and then kept on killing everything she could find. She lived in the forest and took delight in causing fear and pain.

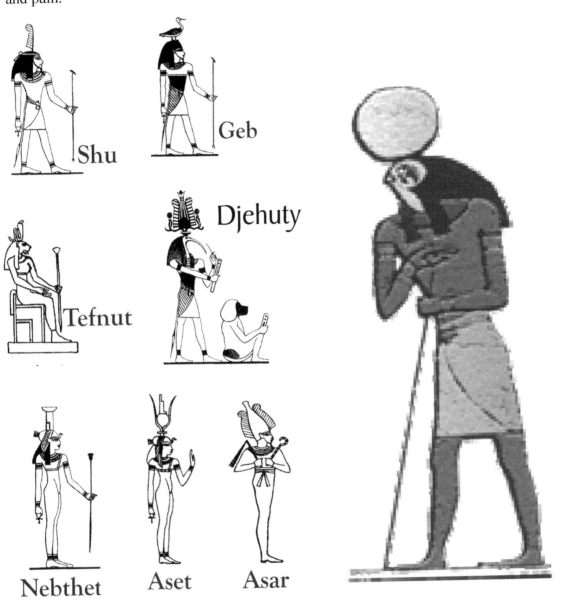

Ra called the company of gods and goddesses and asked who would bring his beautiful daughter back.     Everyone was afraid because as the Eye of Ra, Hetheru held the power of life and death over all things. Ra sent the god Geb to bring Hetheru back. But when he tried to speak to her she almost killed and ate Geb so Geb reported to Ra that she was out of control and even with his powers he could not control her and he was afraid. In her new form Hetheru lived the life of a predator. She hunted and killed anything that came into her view without discrimination or remorse. So Ra called the god Djehuty and asked him to find and bring back the beautiful Hetheru. Djehuty realized that if he was to

51

accomplish this dangerous task he would need to be clever in order to avoid being Hetheru's next meal.

Djehuty transformed himself into the form of a harmless baboon and then he set out to find Hetheru. In order to calm her before approaching her a special drink was given to her as a sedative so that Djehuty would not become her next victim. The drink was to be placed in a location where she could find it. Since she now enjoyed eating people it was thought best to provide her with a drink containing blood but with some extra ingredients. The extra ingredients were beer and mandrake. This drink is called **Setjert.** It is a preparation that allowed her to decrease the intensity of worldly desires, to find a place of calmness within which to recover partially her intellectual capacity and regain some self-control and thereby have an opportunity to reason more clearly and listen to the wisdom of Djehuty.

He found Hetheru sitting alone, licking her paws. He crept closer to her and made noise to announce his approach. When Hetheru realized that something was approaching she immediately took an offensive stance and prepared to fight. Then Djehuty called out, "Hail O beautiful daughter of the Sun!" As soon as Hetheru noticed that it was only a baboon she took poise and immediately Djehuty asked if he could speak with her.

53

## *THE FIRST PARABLE*

Hetheru replied, "Say what you have to say and then I will eat you." Then Djehuty replied, "You certainly have the power to kill me, but you should think about the parable of the vulture and the wildcat."

Hetheru instructed him, "What is this parable? Tell me right now," and then she sat down. Djehuty began to speak immediately so as to keep her attention captivated with interest,

"There was a mother vulture and a mother wildcat who were close neighbors. The vulture had four chicks and the wildcat had given birth to four kittens. The mother vulture and the mother wildcat had a big problem. Their children were hungry but the two mothers were both afraid to leave them alone because they feared that either one of them would kill the other's children for food.

The mothers arranged a truce between them by swearing an oath upon the name of Ra. They swore that neither one would hurt the other's children. So now they both felt secure enough to go out and start hunting food for their children. For some time the truce worked, and soon the vulture chicks and the kittens began to grow.

One day, one of the vulture chicks went to the area where the kittens were playing. He snatched away a portion of their food. One of the kittens reached out and swatted the chick, injuring it, and told it to find its own food. The chick could not fly but had enough strength to tell the kitten, "you have broken the oath between our families and Ra will punish you for this great injustice."

When the mother vulture returned she noticed that her chick was lying on the ground so she figured that the wildcat had broken her promise. The next time that the wildcat left to go hunting the mother vulture killed all of the kittens and brought them back to her nest for food.

When the mother wildcat returned she realized that the mother vulture had killed her kittens, so she cried out to Ra, "O Divine one who upholds justice and righteousness, punish the evil doer who has broken the oath which was sworn upon your name!" Ra heard this plea and set the plan in motion to carry out the punishment for this transgression.

The next day as the mother vulture was hunting she came upon a campfire which had a portion of meat being cooked and there was no one in sight. She swooped down and grabbed it and quickly returned to her nest and dropped it there for her chicks to feast on. She had not noticed that there was a smoldering piece of coal attached to the meat. The nest caught fire and the three chicks were burnt to death. Noticing this the mother wildcat yelled out, "You killed my children and now Ra has punished you!"

Djehuty explained, "Oh Glorious Lady (Hetheru) do you see the omniscience and justice of Ra, who sees and hears all things? He is the giver of life and all of nature owes its existence to him. He controls every particle of Creation. He is the sustainer of Creation. His justice is perfect. Praises be to him and praises be to you who are his daughter!"

Hetheru began to reflect upon the meaning of this parable and she began to remember her father and the wonderful relationship they shared in the past.

Djehuty took advantage of the opportunity and moved closer to her and said, "Oh Divine Lady, I bring you an offering of divine food from the abode of the Sun god (Ra). It brings health and joy to all who eat it."

56

Hetheru began to relax and saw no harm in accepting the tribute from the humble baboon.

## THE DIVINE OFFERING AND THE WISDOM ABOUT THE ORIGINS OF CREATION

In Kemetic culture and spirituality, the divine offering, the *arit,* is a eucharist which embodies the Divine spirit. The highest arit is the Divine eye. As the beautiful goddess, now in her lioness form, consumed the offering Djehuty began to speak again, "These herbs come from the land of Egypt. Egypt is the land which rose up from the Nun, the Primeval Waters, in ancient times. It was created for the gods and goddesses. It is also the home of your Divine Father and your brother Shu. All beings long to return to the land of their birth. Who can be happy living away from the very source of happiness where they were born?"

Hetheru had forgotten her true identity and had become addicted to the taste of blood. Now she began to remember the wonder of her Divine Father, Egypt and her own true identity. She began to think about her temples in Egypt and how men and women had brought her offerings and revered her beauty as the most exalted of all goddesses. Hetheru was so overwhelmed by these memories and feelings that she began to cry.

Djehuty spoke again, "Oh Great Lady, you are crying now but think of the pain of the people in Egypt who are deprived of your glories. Due to your absence there is no merriment, no singing, no parties in Egypt, and the evil doers are going unpunished. Return with me and I will tell you more stories of Egypt."

As soon as she heard this Hetheru realized that he was trying to get her to go back to Egypt and she became exceedingly angry. She growled and made terrible sounds and Djehuty immediately prostrated himself and begged for mercy in the name of Ra, "Oh Divine Lady, before you kill me listen to this important parable about the two vultures."

## THE SECOND PARABLE

Hetheru calmed down because she was intrigued by the words of Djehuty. He quickly began to speak. "Once upon a time there were two vultures in the forest. One said to the other, "My eyes are so perfect that I can see all things to the end of the earth." The other vulture said, "Well I can hear everything. I can even hear Ra as he decrees the fate of all Creation."

The two vultures debated about which gift is better. The vulture with the keen hearing said, "Another bird far away told him that an fly was eaten by a lizard. The lizard was then eaten by a snake and then the snake was caught by a hawk. The snake was so heavy that the snake and the hawk fell into the sea. Can you tell me what is happening now by looking with your keen eyesight?"

The vulture with the keen eyesight replied, "The hawk and the snake have been swallowed by a fish and that fish was swallowed up by a larger fish.

59

The bigger fish came to close to shore and a lion grabbed it out of the sea. Then a legendary creature called *Sefer* (Sfr) or griffin (English) flew to the area and carried off the lion.

One vulture said to the other, "This remarkable scene that we have witnessed proves the power of Ra. Even the existence of the fly was noticed, and the consequence of killing will be punished by one's own death. But how is it that the Sefer has survived all of this?" The other vulture answered, "It must be that the Sefer is the messenger of Ra who was sent out to carry out the law of Ra. The Sefer is the most powerful of all creatures."

So Djehuty began to explain the moral of the parable, "Oh Great Lady, do you see how the Divine Father rewards goodness with goodness and evil with evil? In this manner the balance of the universe is maintained by the Great God. Oh Great Lady, you have been endowed with Ra's power. You are the Eye of Ra. You have the power to carry out the law of Ra. You are the most powerful force in all of Creation."

After hearing this the goddess' eyes filled with joy and she began to feel pride in being the daughter of Ra. She told Djehuty, "You may now relax, humble one, I no longer desire to kill and eat you. Your words have captivated me and I know that you are a beneficent being." They began to walk towards Egypt and Djehuty began to recite another parable.

### THE THIRD PARABLE

Djehuty began, "Once upon a time there were two jackals who were great friends. One day, as they rested, suddenly they saw a lion running towards them. Much to the lion's surprise they did not attempt to run away. When the lion reached them it stopped and asked them why they did not try to run away. The jackals replied that the lion would catch them anyway so there was no point in running away and getting tired in a futile effort to escape. The lion was so pleased with their calm and truthful answer that he spared their life.

Djehuty said to Hetheru, "Let us walk towards Egypt and I will protect you on the way." Hetheru raised her eyebrow at him as soon as she heard this and replied, "How can you protect me? The Eye of the Sun is the most powerful force and it needs no protection, especially from a baboon!"

Djehuty replied, "The strong sometimes need help from those who are weaker. Do you recall the parable of the mouse and the lion? I will tell you."

## *THE FOURTH PARABLE*

Djehuty began to tell the parable as they walked towards Egypt. "There was a lion who lived as a king. He was so powerful that all the other animals feared him. One day the lion came upon a panther who was badly wounded. The lion asked the panther who had injured him and the panther told him that man was responsible for his injuries. The lion never heard of an animal called man.

He decided to hunt man. On the way to find man the lion met a mule, an ox, a cow, a bear and another lion. All of them had been outsmarted by man even though they were more powerful than man. They all said that man was the most cunning creature even though he appeared to be feeble and weak. They told the powerful lion to stay away from man. This only made the lion more determined to find man.

On the way the lion came across a small mouse. Without a thought the lion raised a paw to crush the mouse but the mouse pleaded for mercy and pledged to be the lion's friend in his time of need. The lion asked him, "How can you ever help me? I am more powerful than any creature." The mouse replied, "Do not be so sure of yourself. Sometimes the weak can help the powerful." The lion let him go and went on his way.

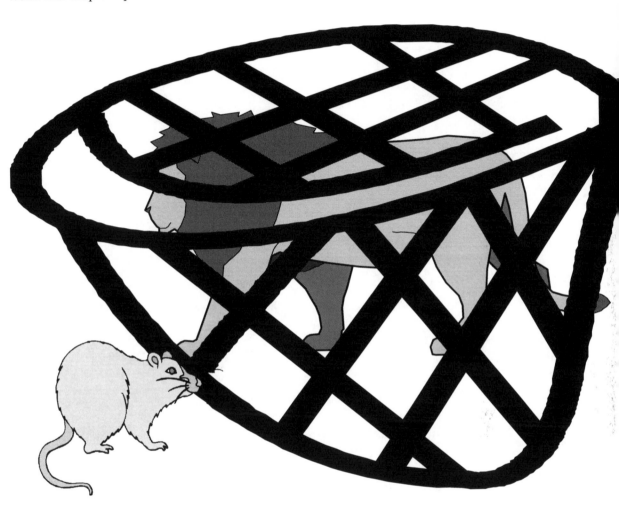

Soon after the encounter with the mouse the lion fell into a pit and was tangled up in a net so strongly that he could not escape. The lion expected to die the next day when man would find him. The lion heard a screeching little voice. It was the little mouse. The mouse worked upon the ropes all night, and before man could come to check the net, the lion had been freed from the death trap. So Great Lady," Djehuty began, "every power will someday meet a higher power and the weak can sometimes help those who are strong."

# *CONCLUSION*

As they entered Egypt the goddess was met with praises from the people who were rejoicing at her return. Before entering the city of Waset (Thebes), Hetheru laid down to rest. She fell asleep and the watchful eye of Djehuty looked after her as she withdrew into the land of slumber.

The enemies of Ra were not pleased with her return so they plotted against her. In the middle of the night they sent a serpent of chaos to poison her in order to leave Ra defenseless, deprived of his protecting Eye. However, Djehuty, who was vigilant all of the time, noticed

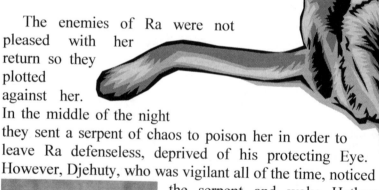

the serpent and woke Hetheru. Still in the form of a wildcat, Hetheru leaped on the serpent and broke the serpent's back. She was grateful to Djehuty and recalled the wonderful parable of the mouse and the lion. She knew now that everything that Djehuty had said was true.

64

In the city of Waset there was a great feast in her honor which lasted for seven days. Hetheru was so gratified that she transformed into the form of a beautiful, soothing, gentle and kind woman. Then she and Djehuty continued to move Northward. They reached the sacred city of *Anu* (Heliopolios), the home of Ra. Also, there was rejoicing in the city of *Het-ka-Ptah* [Memphis]. When Hetheru and Ra held each other once again all of the gods and goddesses rejoiced. Djehuty transformed himself back into his original form and then Hetheru recognized him and her heart looked on him with love and gratitude.

65

# Part 2: A Gloss on the Story of Hetheru and Djehuty

**What is enlightenment?**

Enlightenment is the ultimate discovery of life: Who am I? Why am I here? And What can I do to experience glory, peace, contentment, joy and immortality in life and the hereafter!

**What are the Five Steps to Enlightenment?**

In the Ancient Egyptian scripture of Hetheru and Djehuty, five principles are set forth by the Ancient Egyptian Sages. These principles are designed to lead a human being to Spiritual Enlightenment. They are:

**Ignorance**
**The Spiritual Preceptor**
**The Wisdom of Self Knowledge**
**Maat**
**Meditation**

## Control of the Mind

> *The body belongs to the earth and the soul belongs to heaven.*
> —Ancient Egyptian Proverb

The goal of Sema {Yoga} practice is to calm the movements of the Mind because when the mind is calm it is only then that the true nature of the self can be known just as the bottom of a lake can be seen when the silt settles out of the water. The mind is not the essence of a human being but only a tool used by a human being. Its functions are *memory, imagination, intellectualizing (cognizing), and sleep*. These functions are based on mental impressions gathered from previous actions and they operate through the three states of *Lucidity, Agitation, and Dullness*. The functions of the mind leave impressions in the unconscious. When there are too many impressions of individuality and not enough impressions of one's true nature, a person has fallen into delusion and ignorance of self. When the soul comes into physical existence it needs mind in order to interact with the world. If it gets caught up in the mind and its functions and forgets itself it is said to be in the state of ignorance. It is caught up in the cycle of karmic entanglement. Impressions of experiences cause desires, desires cause worldly thoughts, thoughts cause actions and these actions leave new worldly impressions to fuel the process all over again indefinitely, even impelling the soul to reincarnate again and again, perpetuating the delusion. So the process means controlling *Actions, Thoughts, and Desires* so as to promote new impressions of Maat (truth) and thereby a cleansing of the mind, which will lead to desires of truth, thoughts of truth and actions of truth, mental purity and spiritual enlightenment, that is, knowing the true Self.

## THE PHILOSOPHY OF MIND

### *The Goddess Het-Heru*

In a text from the Temple at Dier al-Medina, Hetheru is referred to as having the same divine attributes as Heru. She is described as *"The Golden One"* and *"The Queen of the Gods."* Her shrines being even more numerous than those of Heru, Hetheru or *Het-Heru,* meaning *"The House of Heru"* and *"The House Above* (sky)," became identified, like Heru, with the salvation of the initiate. In the *Egyptian Book of Coming Forth By Day,* she is the one who urges the initiate to do battle with the monster Apep so as not to lose his / her heart as she cries out: *"Take your armor."* In a separate papyrus, the initiate is told that she (Hetheru) is the one who *will make your face perfect among the Gods; she will open your eye so that you may see every day... she will make your legs able to walk with ease in the Underworld. Her name is Hetheru, Lady of Amenta.*

Hetheru represents the power of Ra, the Supreme Spirit, therefore, associating with her implies coming into contact with the boundless source of energy which sustains the universe. Making contact with Hetheru implies the development of inner will-power which engenders clarity of vision to discern what is righteous from what is unrighteous. A mind which is constantly distracted and beset with fetters (anger, hatred, greed, conceit, covetousness, lust, selfishness, etc.) cannot discern the optimal course in life. It becomes weak willed because the negative emotions and feelings drain the mental energy, thus unrighteous actions and sinful thoughts arise and the weak mind cannot resist them. Unrighteous actions lead to adverse situations and adverse situations lead to pain and sorrow in life. (See *Resurrecting Osiris* and *Egyptian Tantra Yoga* for more on Hetheru and the teachings of Egyptian Tantra Yoga.)

In mystical philosophy, the eyes are understood to be the seat of waking consciousness. When you wake someone you look at their eyes to see if they are awake. The right Eye in particular is seen as the dynamic aspect of consciousness. Hetheru, as the right Eye of Ra, symbolizes exactly that concept. God (Ra) has projected consciousness (the Eye) into Creation, and in so doing, the Eye (waking consciousness) becomes involved in various activities within the world of time and space. Similarly, the human soul has projected its image into time and space (the ocean of Creation), and in so doing, the psycho-physical self has emerged and human experience is possible. From this process arises the possibility of karmic involvement as well as ignorance and egoism.

## Hetheru as the Eye of Ra

There are several Ancient Egyptian myths relating to the *"Eye."* One tells that the Eye left Ra and went into Creation and was lost. Ra (Divine Self) sent Djehuty (wisdom) to find the Eye (individual soul) and bring it back. It was through the *magic* (wisdom teachings) of the god Djehuty that the Eye realized who it was and agreed to return to Ra. Upon its return, however, it found that Ra had replaced it with another. In order to pacify it, Ra placed it on his *brow* in the form of a *Uraeus serpent, where it could rule the world.* One variation to the story holds that the Eye left Ra and went to Nubia in the form of a lioness (Hetheru, in her aspect as destroyer of evil and unrighteousness). When Ra heard this, he sent the Nubian god, *Ari-Hems-Nefer* (a form of Shu), and Djehuty to bring the Eye back. They took the form of baboons (symbol of wisdom) and soon found the Eye near the Mountain of the Sunrise, where Asar was born. The Eye refused to leave because it learned to enjoy its new existence. It was destroying those who had committed sins (plotted against Ra) while on earth. Djehuty worked his magic on the Eye and brought it back to Ra. Another variation of the story holds that Ra sent *Shu* and *Tefnut* in search of the Eye. The Eye resisted, and in the struggle, shed tears, and from the tears grew men and women. This is a clever play on words because the word for "tears," Remtu, ⬭ 𓄿 𓂋 𓏤𓏤, (that fell from the eyes of Ra) and the word for "men," Reth or Rethu, ⬭ 𓂋 𓀀 𓏥𓏤, have similar sounds in Ancient Egyptian language. This play on words sustains the idea that human beings came forth out of the sorrow of God as he saw souls leaving him and becoming human beings (i.e. individuals separate from the Divine Self).

The relationship of "tears" to "men" symbolizes the idea that humankind is the expression of the desire of the Divine Self to have experiences in the realm of time and space. Further, "tears" are a symbol of human experience. It implies that human experience is a sorrowful condition because consciousness has degraded itself to the level of gross, limited human experience in the form of an individual ego as opposed to its expansive, limitless Self. This contraction in consciousness is what allows the ego to emerge as an individual and distinct personality out of "nowhere," just as a dream personality emerges out of "nowhere." Instead of knowing itself as the immutable soul, the soul sees the ego and the world of time and space as the reality. This development would be like the ocean forgetting that it is the ocean and believing itself to be one of the waves. Therefore, instead of seeing itself as encompassing all the waves, it is concerned with its transient experience, as an individual wave, and with comparing itself to other waves.

Life is "sorrowful" from the standpoint of wisdom because even conditions that appear to be pleasurable are in reality setting the individual up for disappointment and frustration later on, because no positive situation can last indefinitely. Also, the pursuit of worldly pleasure and pain sets up mental impressions that will survive the death of the body and lead the soul to further incarnations in search of fulfillment. Therefore, the Sages say that *all life is painful to the wise.* This is why Sema {Yoga} philosophy emphasizes going beyond both pleasure *and* pain in order to transcend the bondage to time and space. This can be accomplished by turning away from the world which is illusory and seeking to discover the Self.

The masses of people who do not have spiritual sensitivity put up with the world and its ups and downs due to lack of reflectiveness. Having been taught from their youth by family and society to look for happiness in the world, they do not know any better. Through the development of wisdom and reflection, the aspirant can develop an intuition which transcends pleasure and pain move beyond the world of ordinary human experience as a source of happiness.

Through the story of the Eye, very important mystical teachings are being conveyed. The Eye, *Udjat,* is a symbol of intuitional vision. Also, it represents the desire of the Divine to go into itself (Creation) and the subsequent forgetfulness that ensues. The resistance of the Eye to return to the divine abode is a symbol of the predicament of ordinary people who, through ignorance and intense desire, detest the idea of even considering the spiritual values of life because their hearts (minds) are consumed with passion. They are consumed with the desire to experience the pleasures of material existence. Ra sent the Eye (consciousness) into Creation. Consciousness then became "lost" in Creation, symbolizing the souls of human beings and all life forms, forgetting their true nature. The Eye, lost in Creation, is the human soul which is caught up in the cycle of birth-death-birth (reincarnation) due to forgetfulness and distraction (ignorance of its true nature). The Supreme Being (Ra) sent out the messenger of wisdom (Djehuty) in the forms of *Metu Neter* (ancient scriptures of wisdom) and *Sbai* (spiritual preceptor-Guru) to instruct the Eye in reference to its true nature. Having "remembered" who it was in reality, the Eye then returned to its rightful place.

## Hetheru as a Metaphor

Hetheru represents the predicament of human life. From a state of unity with the Divine (Ra) she becomes degraded to the point of forgetting her true identity. She engages in violent acts and lives out of the lower nature and base desires. This is known as the state of **Dullness of Mind**. The more a person separates from their essential nature, the more a person slides downward into egoism and the lower aspects of the mind which include vices such as anger, hatred, greed, lust, jealousy, etc. Oftentimes these feelings are so strong that they cloud the intellect and render a person incapable of higher forms of thought or feeling. In her aspect as "The Eye of Ra" Hetheru is the highest power. She is the object of awe and admiration for all. But when her mind was degraded, the same awesome power becomes the object of tremendous fear because it is uncontrolled and destructive.

Once again, all human beings have the power to act with great goodness or extremely evil intent. If a person acts out of Maat (virtues such as compassion, non-violence, truth, universal love, harmony, sharing, etc.) then their capacity for goodness is boundless. However, if a person acts out of vices (listed above), then their capacity for negativity is immense even to the extent of self-destruction. When negativity becomes so intense in the mind, the power of thinking is not the only aspect that becomes impaired. A person's memory and identity becomes impaired as well. Instead of seeing herself as the beautiful goddess of light and the enforcer of truth and justice, Hetheru saw herself as the vicious wildcat of death. In the same manner people have forgotten their identity as gods and goddesses and have come to regard themselves as miserable human beings caught in the struggle of life for survival, in competition with other human beings and with nature itself.

Djehuty took on the task of saving Hetheru from the pit of negativity and ignorance into which she had fallen. Djehuty, a symbol of the Spiritual Preceptor, represents the intellect, right thinking and truth.

Sehu Djehuty, Sebai Djehuty

Djehuty is the god of learning, writing, mathematics and language. Djehuty is referred to as Thoth by the Greeks. In Ancient Egyptian mythology, he is the scribe of the gods. He appears as the record keeper of the dead in the *Books of Coming Forth By Day*. He is the patron of learning and of the arts. He is the inventor of writing, and in the specific theology related to him, he is also seen as the Creator of the universe. Djehuty is depicted as a man with the head of a baboon or an ibis bird. He also bears pen and ink, and sometimes also the lunar disk and crescent.

The ibis is a wading bird related to the stork and the heron. The choice of the ibis indicates a unique feature or quality which spiritual learning requires. This quality is related to the *wading* nature of the ibis. Wading means *walking in or through a substance, as water, that offers resistance, impedes or makes movement difficult*. Djehuty represents intellect, the mind and its capacity to cut (wade) through the myriad of thoughts and concepts (water-ocean of consciousness) in order to get to the truth.

The crescent moon symbol of Djehuty is a figure of the moon in its first quarter. It has concave* and convex** edges terminating in points. The crescent moon symbol signifies growing or increasing understanding, reason and spiritual wisdom. Therefore, Djehuty is the embodiment of knowledge. This is one of the reasons why he is said to have created writing. He is also the messenger of Ra who brings the special words of power to Aset in the Asarian Resurrection Story in order for Aset to resurrect Heru. In this aspect he symbolizes the Spiritual Preceptor who brings the wisdom of the Divine Self to the aspirant so the aspirant can resurrect his\her spiritual aspiration. (*Curved like the inner surface of a sphere. **Curved outward, as the exterior of a sphere.)

The universe is understood to be like an ocean of matter through which Ra sails on his barque in order to sustain Creation. Djehuty is Ra's mind, the cosmic mind, with which Ra moves through the ocean of Creation. Thus, the universe is known as an ocean of consciousness called Nu or Nun. The spirit (Ra) uses the Cosmic Mind (Djehuty) to create the objects and varied forms of Creation and maintain order in Creation. Therefore, matter (Creation) is in reality consciousness (Primeval Ocean) which has taken on forms (physical objects) in accordance with the will of the Cosmic Mind. The Cosmic Mind also brings forth learning and knowledge to Creation through the arts, sciences and language. Nothing is invented by human beings. Everything that is created by civilization comes from the Cosmic Mind, and not from any individual human being. To believe otherwise would be egoistic thought. The more a person is in tune with the Cosmic Mind the more knowledge he or she can obtain and the more inner peace and fulfillment a person can experience. The farther away a person gets from the Cosmic mind through negative actions, ignorance and delusion, the less able a person is to discover goodness, inner peace, knowledge, happiness and health in life.

# The Moon is the Symbol of The Mind

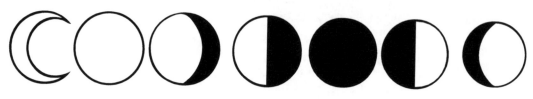

**The Moon (Djehuty) is the reflection of the Sun (Ra) and as such it waxes and wanes (It receives energy from the sun but not in fullness. It** fluctuates)

The Mind is a reflection of the Self or Spirit (God). Due to impurities (anger, hatreds, greed, etc.) in the mind its ability receive wisdom, fulfillment, inner peace and happiness fluctuates.

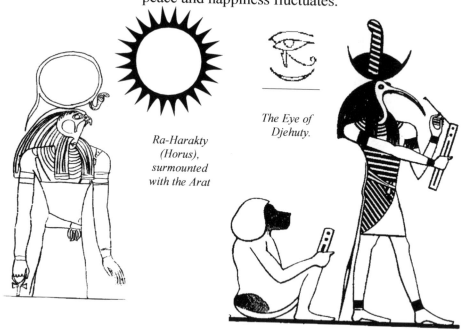

*Ra-Harakty (Horus), surmounted with the Arat*

*The Eye of Djehuty.*

So Djehuty devises a plan to approach Hetheru. Understanding that she is in a state of intense *dullness,* he knows that he cannot approach her directly by using his ordinary form and by giving her direct teachings as to the nature of the Self (Ra) and her true identity (Hetheru, the Eye of Ra). So he decides to transform himself into the form of a humble, harmless looking baboon instead of presenting himself in the form of a regal ibis headed divinity. It would be very difficult for an ordinary person to behold and accept the real form of the Divine Self (Supreme Being). Therefore, the indirect means of religion, yoga, symbols, myth and parables are adopted until a spiritual aspirant is ready to have a direct experience. At that time the indirect means are placed aside in order to experience the Divine who transcends all forms, concepts, religions and symbols. So Djehuty decided to present to Hetheru some of the most profound teachings related to the nature of the Self in the form of parables in order to gradually gain her confidence and stimulate her latent memories of her own true glory.

In the beginning, the Spiritual Preceptor must help the individual to somehow turn the anguish and pain experienced as a result of interaction with the world into a desire to rise above it. To this end, a series of techniques and disciplines have been developed over thousands of years. Some of these methods are myths, parables, mental disciplines, meditation and physical culture (Sema {Yoga} exercises and development of the internal Life Force). The teacher needs to help the seeker to restructure and channel those energies which arise from disappointment and frustration into a healthy dispassion for the illusoriness of the world and its entanglements. The teacher shows the way to develop spiritual aspiration and self-effort directed at sustaining a viable personal spiritual program or *Sheti*.

Djehuty is the quintessential image of the Guru in this story. The word "Guru" is an Indian Sanskrit term meaning "Spiritual Preceptor," a teacher of spiritual truths. A Spiritual Preceptor is a Sage who shows others the way to understand the higher reality beyond the ordinary phenomenal universe. He or she shows others how to discover their true identity and realize their oneness with the Divine. In essence, they are spiritual guides.

In Ancient Egyptian Mythology there are two great Spiritual Preceptors. Djehuty is one of them. He is the wonderful teacher of Hetheru. The other one is Aset. In the Shetaut Asar or The Story of Asar, Aset and Heru otherwise known as the Asarian Resurrection, she is the teacher to her son Heru. She trains him in the arts, sciences and the mystical philosophy of Creation and the nature of the Divine Self. She enables Heru to receive the Divine Vision which she obtained from Ra in the Story of Ra and Aset.

The word **Sehu** is the Ancient Egyptian term meaning "Spiritual Counselor" and **Sebai** means "Spiritual Preceptor". A Spiritual Preceptor is not only a person who has attained a high level of internal self-discovery and purity, but also a person who is well versed in the scriptural writings and has knowledge of parables and myths along with their mystical implications. He or she also knows the practices which lead a person to spiritual evolution (Sema {Yoga} disciplines).

If the teaching is given directly it may be misunderstood or even repudiated altogether due to the state of mind of the individual. Hence, the student must be properly initiated into the teaching and the proper relationship must be established between teacher and student.

The teacher offers humility and honesty with a beguiling wit, cheerfulness and an uplifting outlook. This is symbolized by the divine food Djehuty offered Hetheru. The teacher brings divine food in the form of wisdom teachings which uplift the mind by relieving the burden of pain and sorrow which weighs down the soul of a human being due to ignorance and negativity. The divine food is the taste of divine glory. It is a glimpse of the goal which a disciple must aspire to experience in its fullness. However, this fullness is experienced in degrees as the teacher gives the spiritual teaching and as it is assimilated by the student.

# IMPORTANT: The Healing Power of Djehuty

The Healing Power of Djehuty consists in the liberating vision that results from the wisdom teaching and culminates in restoring the condition of the Eye (Human Consciousness) to its state before the impurities (ignorance about the Higher Self, anger, hatred, greed, lust, etc.) came in.

Figure 17: Tehuti restoring to Horus the Udjat (Uatchit) Eye, 𓂀, which Set had blinded.

Thus Djehuty speaks:

*"I came seeking the Eye of Heru , that I might bring it back and count it. I found it (now it is) complete, counted and sound, so that it can flame up to the sky and blow above and below..."*

The name for the Eye of Heru may be pronounced as *"Wedjat"*, *"Udjat" or "Utchat"* meaning: *"the whole or restored one"* and also *"that which protects."*

Djehuty restores the eye through writings which bring wisdom, right thinking, right acting and these lead to freedom from stress and mental imbalance. Freedom from stress allows the energy of the spirit to course freely though the mind and body and enlightenment.

Djehuty is an Ibis, a wading bird. Wading birds have a special capacity to move through water and probe for specific items they desire with their long beaks. The world is the ocean of consciousness and Djehuty is the aspect of the mind that can navigate through the world with healthy reasoning, vigor and intuition.

The student must learn to respect and trust the teacher. Also, the student must allow the teaching to penetrate deeply within the heart. It is only then that the teaching will have a transformative effect. Hetheru allowed Djehuty's words to penetrate her cold, anguished heart. Then she began to remember her past glory. This is the process of divine memory wherein she began to regain the remembrance of her true identity. The pain of seeing her current level of existence in comparison with her past glory brought her to tears. Also, she felt the pain of realizing that she was missing out on the boundless divine love of her father. This is the common emotional experience of a spiritual aspirant when understanding as to their true predicament begins to dawn. "What have I done to come down from the heights of divinity to the limited state of human life and mortal existence? How wretched am I? How degraded am I?" These are the kinds of questions asked by a spiritual aspirant before he / she begins to understand the meaning of the spiritual teachings. This form of thinking leads to a resolution to regain one's true glory and to rise up from the degradation of ignorance, "May I find a teacher who can guide me on the path to self-discovery and enlightenment at once!" Thus, Hetheru, came to respect Djehuty. She accepted his offering, listened to his teaching and later trusted him with her life. As one begins to reflect on the teaching, intuitional understanding opens up the opportunity to view the beauty and experience the infinite compassion of the Self. Then there are no more questions, only a keen desire to experience this elevated state more and more. An aspirant might say at this point, "I have glimpsed a wondrous bliss within. Let me fully discover it and abide in it."

## The First Parable imparted the understanding of

*Maat* or truth, balance, cuase and effect, righteous action [*ari*] and the glory of the Divine. Maat is the order, justice and righteousness of the universe. It is the law of cause and effect set up by the Divine to maintain harmony in the universe. Any action performed will bring a reaction to the person performing the action. Thus, positive actions set up a positive karmic basis for positive occurences in a person's life. Negative actions set up a negative karmic basis for negative occurences to happen in a person's life. It may not be right away but it will occur at some point in time. Therefore, it is important to hold pure thoughts and perform good deeds in order to promote goodness, peace and harmony in your life. What you do comes back to you! This is the Ancient Egyptian **Principle of Meskhenet**. This principle of **Meskhenet** relates to what in popular culture is most commonly refered to as Karma and Reincarnation.

What is Ari? The answer to this questions can be found in the *Ru Pert Em Heru* texts or "Book of Enlightenment" (also incorrectly known as the Book of the Dead, Book of Coming Forth by Day). The goddess *Meskhent* presides over the future birth of an individual but she represents only the culmination of the process, which has come to be known as *Uhm-Ankh* "reincarnation" in modern times. In reality it is the individual who determines his or her own fate by the actions they perform in life. However, the wisdom of the ancient Egyptian Sages dictated that the process should be explained in mythological terms to help people better understand the philosophy. The process works as follows:

The divinities *Shai* 𓀭𓏜 𓀭𓏤 and 𓊃𓊃𓏏 *Renunut* govern an individual's fate or destiny and their fortune. These deities are the hands of the great god Djehuty (he symbolizes the intellectual development of a human being) and he inscribes a person's fate once they have faced the scales of Maat, that is, they are judged in reference to their past ability to uphold Maat in life. A person's intellectual capacity reflects in their actions. Thus, it is fitting for the intellect to judge its own actions. Further, God does not judge anyone because we are all essentially gods and goddesses, sparks of the same divinity, so God within us judges us. This is an objective judgment which only the individual is responsible for and it occurs at the unconscious level of the mind, beyond any interference from a persons personality or ego consciousness which is on the surface level of the mind; therefore, one's conscious desire to go to heaven at the time of death or one's conscious repentance at the time of death for misdeeds in life cannot overcome the weight of the 𓂀 *ari* – (action thing done make something deed *Ari* -Karma) one has set up during a lifetime. So it is important to begin now to purify the heart and cleanse the soul so as to become 𓂝𓊪𓏤𓆣 **or** 𓐩 *Maakheru* (true of speech-pure of heart) at the time of the judgment. The gods and goddesses are cosmic forces which only facilitate the process but from a mythological and philosophical standpoint they are concepts for understanding the mystical philosophy of the teaching.

Once the judgment has been rendered the goddess *Meskhent* takes over and appoints the person's future family, place of birth, social status, etc. This is not meant as a punishment but as a process of leading the soul to the appropriate place where they can grow spiritually. If before you died you desired to be a musician the goddess will send you to a country, family and circumstances where this desire can be pursued. If you were a mugger in a past life you will end up in a place and situation where you will experience pain and suffering such as you caused to others and this experience will teach you to act otherwise in the future, thus improving your future birth. What you do after that is within the purview of your own free will and your actions in this new lifetime will engender and determine the next, and on and on. This process is 𓉐𓈖𓏏 *Meskhent*- "destiny of birth." Meskhent is the manifestation of one's *shai-nefer* 𓀭𓄤𓏤, positive destiny, or one's *shai-mit* 𓀭𓅱𓏤𓅆, negative destiny. This is ones harvest 𓊃𓊃𓏏 or what one reaps from one's actions.

This is the process leading to *Uhm Ankh* (reincarnation). The objective is to lead oneself on a process of increasingly better births until it is possible to have spiritual inclination and the company of Sages and Saints who can lead a person to self-discovery ( 𓂋𓐍𓏤𓄤 *Rech-ab*). When a person achieves this self-discovery they are referred to as *Akh* 𓅜 (the enlightened).

Alltogether, the sum total of a person's past actions, desires, feelings, thoughts and belief system is considered the person's *ariu*. (popularly known as The Law of Karma in modern culture)

First, a person must become virtuous because this purifies the person's actions and thus, their Ari (karmic) basis. Negative Ari leads to negative situations but also to mental dullness and it is hard to understand the teachings when the mind is in a dull state, full of base thoughts, desires and feelings- this is the opposite of *Rech-ab*, it may be referred to as ⸗ *inj-Set* (mind afflicted by fetters of Set). There is much mental agitation and suffering. The positive karmic basis allows harmonious surroundings and birth into the family of spiritually minded people as well as the company of Sages but most importantly the clarity of mind to understand the wisdom teachings. If the soul is judged to be pure in reference to Maat it will not be led to *Uhem Ankh* (reincarnation) but to the inner shrine where it meets its own higher self, i.e. God. Asar, the soul, meets Asar the Supreme Being. This meeting ends any future possibility of reincarnation. It means becoming one with the Divine Self. It is termed

*Nehast* ⸗ (Resurrection), i.e. the Ausarian Resurrection. This is the only way to break the cycle of reincarnation.

So *ari* (karma) is not destiny but the accumulated unconscious impressions from desires, thoughts and feelings of the past (the present and previous lives) and not a set destiny. A person can change their *ari* by their present actions. The individual is always responsible for the present by the actions they performed previously which led them to the place they are today, etc. external factors can affect one's life but one is still in control ultimately of the response to those externalities of life (other people, circumstances, etc.). However, the present is not set. Otherwise people could not change and they would be destined to suffer or be happy based on some perverse cosmic joke and their destiny would be out of their control. It is not like that. God has provided free will and with it a person can have a glorious life full of wisdom and prosperity or a life of strife, suffering and frustration based on egoism and egoistic desires and the actions one chooses.

The Ancient Egyptian word "Meskhent" is based on the word "*Mesken*." *Mesken* ⸗ means birthing place. Thus, *Meskhent* is the goddess (cosmic force) which presides over the *Mesken* of newborn souls. She makes effective, a person's future fate, determined by a person's desires and unconscious inclinations by placing a person who is to reincarnate into the appropriate circumstance for the new life based on previous actions and future potential.

The goddesses *Shai* (fate or destiny), *Rennenet* (fortune) and *Meskhenet* together form the principle of cause and effect which determines a person's future in accordance with their actions, beliefs, feelings and desires, their karmic basis. Therefore, these deities (cosmic forces set up by the Divine) decree whether or not a person will move forward and attain oneness with the Divine or if the person will move backwards and experience degraded states of mind. They determine the next birth (family, country, circumstance, etc.) of an individual. The important thing to understand is that they do not determine a person's fate or destiny. They only carry out the sum total of a person's karmic will.

A person's karmic will is their unconscious resolve based on their accumulated desires, beliefs and feelings by which a person has lived, the karmic basis. So if a person desires wealth and carries out various actions in an attempt to gain wealth they set up a basis for seeking wealth. These actions become stored in the unconscious mind as impressions and at the time of death they impel a person to continue searching for wealth in an unconscious way. If a person was evil in life their own karmic basis will send them to a plane of consciousness where they will suffer evil experiences. This is known as Hell. If a person was a performer of good deeds in life their own karmic basis will send them to a plane of consciousness where they will experience heavenly conditions. This is known as Heaven.

If the person could not attain some desire in the present lifetime, Meskhenet will cause that person to be reborn in a country, family and circumstance where they will be able to continue pursuing that desire (karmic will). This form of desiring things which are ultimately perishable becomes the basis for reincarnation. Heaven and hell are not permanent states of being for the soul. Like the physical world and human life, heaven and hell are relative states. All relative states of experience are transitory. They all come to an end. The only state of being that is permanent and, imperishable is when the mind is enlightened and the eternal Divine Self is discovered. This is because all desires and the entire karmic basis dissolves. Enlightenment dissolves the karmic basis because it is made up of illusions, desires, passions and ignorance. Since spiritual practice and enlightenment eradicates ignorance and illusions, there are no desires left for that which is negative or for the ephemeral pleasures and attainments of mortal existence. If a person was a practitioner of Yoga in life, their own purified karmic basis will send them to expand beyond desires and to discover the Divine Self. This is known as spiritual enlightenment, liberation, eternal freedom, immortality, etc. Only this attainment ends the cycle of birth and death (reincarnation, going back into a body in order to experience physical human existence once again).

Therefore, spiritual philosophy directs a spiritual aspirant to desire after that which is not perishable and fleeting, the Divine Self. So it is important to understand that a person can control his or her own fate by controlling their desires, thoughts and feelings. These put together comprise what is referred to as "mind" in mystical philosophy. Therefore, control of the mind is the most important aspect of spiritual practice because the mind determines everything that happens in life, whether it be positive or negative. Mind is the cause of experiences of hell or heaven, happiness or sorrow, enlightenment or degradation, etc.

Even the most infinitesimal forms of life in the universe cannot escape this karmic law. Therefore, a spiritual aspirant must learn to desire what is true and to act according to what is good and righteous. The karmic law is an example of the power and glory of the Divine Self (Ra). Even more wonderful is the realization that every living being is a part of the intricate fabric of life and that all are looked after by the Supreme Being, no matter how insignificant they may seem to be. Another important teaching here is that no one can do an unrighteous act and get away with it. At some point (in the present life or in a future life) they will reap the effects of their unrighteous action of the past in the form of misfortune, adversity, disappointment and frustrations. Punishment is meted for all those who transgress the universal laws of life which include compassion, honesty, justice, righteousness, peace and universal love.

So the law of karma says that for every cause there will be an effect. In addition, the cause and the effect will be of equal intensity. Also, the effect will be the cause transformed. The problem arises because the majority of people do not have proper insight into this law. Most people do not even believe that they are the only person responsible for the situations that befall them in life, good or bad. However, they are usually more willing to take credit for the good things that happen to them than the bad things. This problem is compounded because often the cause and the effect do not look identical, and do not occur one right after the other. For example, if you plant a seed of a sweet fruit (i.e. date), you will reap sweet fruits. However, if you planted the seed of a sour fruit (i.e. lime), you will reap only sour fruits. So, you will reap the results of whatever thoughts and actions you put out into the world. This reaping is carried over into future lifetimes. However, neither the seed of the date or lime look like the actual fruit it brought forth. If you were only to see the fruit (effect), you may not be able to describe the exact way the seed which was planted (cause) looked. Likewise, most people have no insight into the cause of the negative effect they are currently experiencing in their lives. Therefore, the tendency in modern society is to blame someone or something outside of oneself for any adversity which befalls one. The purpose of having insight into this law is not to blame yourself for your current adverse situations and wallow in self-pity, but to realize that as you created the situation due to ignorant (egoistic) behavior in the past, you can un-create it through righteous thoughts and actions in the present. You are not stuck in your situation indefinitely. Through your righteous self-effort you have every possibility of working to make your situation better. Therefore the purpose of thoroughly understanding the law of cause and effect (Maat philosophy) is to become self-empowered, and not to feel that you are a poor victim of life's cruel whims who has no control over their destiny.

Following the first parable, Djehuty introduces the teachings related to the Creation of the universe. He explains to Hetheru that the land of Egypt was created by her father (Ra) from a Primeval Ocean which was formless in the beginning, and that it is a land of many wonders and incomparable beauty. This description is a mystical way of relating the nature of Creation and the glory of the entity who created it. Then Djehuty begins to show her that the splendor of the Supreme Being is also her own splendor and glory. He begins to relate her to the divine glory that is latent within herself and to bolster her pride in her own heritage. He imparts to her the feeling of goodness that is the Divine. He relates how her absence left a great void in Creation, causing pain and sorrow to all people. Every life form has a place in Creation.

Also, every life form is loved by God, who manifests his love in the form of relatives, acquaintances and nature itself. So all people have a purpose in life and their existence is meaningful. Also, they are cared for by the Divine Self in various forms. The highest purpose is to discover your true identity and find your own place which has been degreed for you by the Supreme Divinity.

# THE PSYCHOMYTHOLOGY OF THE CREATION

Psycho-mythology is the term I have coined to refer to the study of myth as a tool for promoting psychological integration and well being and spiritual evolution. The term *"psycho,"* is to be understood to mean everything that constitutes human consciousness in all of its stages and states, but most importantly, the subconscious and unconscious levels of mind. *"Mythology"* here refers to the study of the codes, messages, ideas, directives, stories, culture, beliefs, etc., that affect the personality through the conscious, subconscious and unconscious aspects of the mind of an individual, specifically those effects which result in psycho-spiritual transformation, that is, a transpersonal or transcendental change in the personality of an individual which leads to the discovery of the transcendental reality behind all existence.

The process of Creation is explained in the form of a cosmological system for better understanding. Cosmology is a branch of philosophy dealing with the origin, processes and structure of the universe. Cosmogony is the astrophysical study of the Creation and evolution of the universe. Both of these disciplines are inherent facets of Egyptian philosophy through the main religious systems or Companies of the gods and goddesses. A company of gods and goddesses is a group of deities which symbolize a particular cosmic force or principle which emanates from the all-encompassing Supreme Being, from which they have emerged. The Self or Supreme Being manifests Creation through the properties and principles represented by the *Pautti* (Company of gods and goddesses-cosmic laws of nature). The system or company of gods and goddesses of Anu is regarded as the oldest, and forms the basis of the Osirian Trinity. It is expressed in the diagram below.

The diagram above shows that *Pautti*, the creative principles which are embodied in the primordial gods and goddesses of Creation, emanated from the Supreme Being. Ra or Ra-Tem arose out of the *"Nu,"* the Primeval waters, the hidden essence, and began sailing the *"Boat of Millions of Years"* which included the company of gods and goddesses. On his boat emerged the "Neteru" or cosmic principles of Creation. The neters of the Pautti are Ra-Atum, Shu, Tefnut, Geb, Nut, Asar, Aset, Set, and Nebthet. Hetheru, Djehuty and Maat represent attributes of the Supreme Being as the very *stuff* or *substratum* which makes up Creation. Shu, Tefnut, Geb, Nut, Asar (Osiris), Aset (Isis), Set, and Nebthet (Nephthys) represent the principles upon which Creation manifests. Apuat or Anubis is not part of the Ennead. He represents the feature of intellectual discrimination in the Osirian myth. "Sailing" signifies the beginning of motion in Creation. Motion implies that events occur in the realm of time and space, thus, the phenomenal universe comes into existence as a mass of moving essence we call the elements. Prior to this motion, there was the primeval state of being without any form and without existence in time or space.

Ra-Tem
⇩
Hetheru
Djehuty
Maat
⇩
Shu ⇔ Tefnut
⇩
Geb⇔Nut

Set — Nebthet    Asar ⇔ Aset    Asar⇔ Nebthet
⇩           ⇩
Heru        Apuat

Hetheru began to cry upon realizing what she seemed to have lost and forgotten. Then a strange thing happened. Djehuty tried to get her to return to Egypt and all of a sudden she realized what he was doing and she fell back into the pit of negativity. This is not an uncommon occurrence in spiritual life or in ordinary life. Sometimes a person may experience joy, and then seemingly for no reason they may fall into the pits of depression. Sometimes the mental delusion and the erupting emotions cause a person to strike out with anger in an uncontrolled manner, even towards those who offer them kindness or the truth. This is a factor caused by negative impressions in the karmic basis from the past. Anger, hatred and rage are forms of mental illness and their intensity most times incapacitates a person's faculties of reasoning self-control. At this time, understanding, gentleness, forgiveness and humility, but most of all patience are needed in order to deal with people who are in this degraded, dull state of mind.

Djehuty is the embodiment of patience and the wellspring of parables (mystical wisdom teachings). So he wisely humbles himself and begs for mercy. He seemingly submits to her power and does not attempt to confront it since he is no match for her might. At the same time he cleverly captivates her attention away from anger and violence and channels her feelings towards interest in another mystical parable. An important point in dealing with the dull mind is how the negative thoughts and feelings are handled. It is important to view the negative thoughts and feelings as well as the adverse conditions of life as challenges to be overcome instead of as feeling that one is a victim of negativity from others or from one's own mistakes. The former idea is empowering because a person who practices it will not allow the negativity to make them upset. When the mind is not upset it can endure the negativity, understanding that it will not last forever, while at the same time think clearly and resolve the problems. Also, it is very important when in a dull state of mind that one should not simply say, "I will wait until the negativity passes over before I do any work" or try to figure out where the negativity came from, because these tactics will only serve to increase the negativity. Suppose you have a hole in the ground you want to go away. If you keep digging the hole, believing that it will either go away or you will be able to find out where it comes from, you will only make the hole bigger. A mind, clouded by agitation and distress, will lead itself into deeper and deeper pits of despair, anguish and sorrow with no resolution in view. The only way to fix the hole is by bringing fresh dirt and filling it. Likewise, when you have the hole of negativity in your consciousness, you must fill it with something opposite to effect a change. So the scriptures recommend the disciplines of prayer, selfless service, repetition of the Divine Name, reflection on scriptural teachings to channel the negative emotions in a positive direction, as exemplified by this story.

In addition, the teaching itself must be presented in a manner to which the aspirant can relate. This objective is accomplished through the use of myths, parables, stories, similes and metaphors which are directly relevant to an individual's cultural experience and their human experience. *Listening to the teachings* is the first and most important step in the process of spiritual transformation. Therefore, many intriguing, fascinating and beguiling ways have been devised by the Sages to transmit the teachings that captivate the attention of the listener. Myths and parables have very important features. They are easier to recall, and have a more direct impact on the untrained mind than direct mystical philosophy because they are easy to identify with, as opposed to proverbs or aphorisms which contain raw spiritual truths that require a well trained mind in order to be grasped and appreciated. The next step in the process of learning the teachings it *reflecting* upon them. This implies the continuous study and practice of the teachings. As you read over a spiritual text and practice its wisdom in your life, deeper and deeper aspects of the teaching will reveal themselves to you, purifying your heart in greater and greater degrees. The next step in learning the teachings is *meditating* upon them. Meditation implies going deep within your mind to a level which is beyond thoughts and senses. It is discovering the *intuitional* level of mind. The correct understanding of the teachings and their continuous practice in day to day life will automatically lead a person to the meditative state in the course of time. This level of mind is also known in Ancient Egyptian terminology as *Nrutef,* the place where there are no thoughts or mental vibrations. This practice means communing with the absolute Self within you which is beyond your thoughts, desires and sentimental feelings.

## The Second Parable

The Second Parable reinforces the teaching of Ra's omniscience. Hetheru was able to develop *devotion towards the Divine.* Devotion towards the Divine is an important development in spiritual life. It means channeling one's emotions towards what is true, beautiful and good and turning away from that which is erroneous, illusory and the source of pain and sorrow in life. So devotion to God means turning away from the sentimental desires of the ego and turning the feelings toward the Divine. Devotion and wisdom are closely related. Each fulfills the other and together they lead a spiritual aspirant to discover the Higher Self. In order to love something, you must learn about it. The Divine Self is no exception. The blossoming devotion in Hetheru's heart (love for God) and the teaching of Djehuty about the wisdom of the Self allowed Hetheru to calm down and to see the infinite glory of the Divine Self. His teachings revealed the hierarchical order of living beings in Creation, and also the idea that even the most powerful living beings are all under the control of and ultimately answer to the Supreme Self.

Djehuty presents the character of the Ancient Egyptian Sefer (griffin) in the role of divine avenger or the divinity who enforces the divine law. The griffin is a mythological animal encompassing the body of a lion, the head and wings of a hawk, and the tail of a lion or a serpent. In legends from India, the

Far East and ancient Scythia, griffins were known as the guardians of treasures and mines. In Greek mythology they drew the carriage or chariot of the sun and were the guardians of gold treasures. In this parable the Sefer represents the supreme instrument or power of the Divine. In reality, this is Hetheru's true identity as the Eye of Ra. This is why Djehuty created an elaborate story detailing the hierarchy of creatures and showing how none can escape from the power of the Sefer. So in a subtle and indirect way he is teaching her about herself throughout the story. At the end of the parable he reveals to her that she has this same power and that she herself is the Eye of Ra which has power over all creatures. Thus, he introduces her to her own higher nature in a clever and artistic manner.

Another important teaching presented to Hetheru in the first two parables was that of *faith.* The teaching showed her how God exists in the very fabric of Creation. In fact all Creation has proceeded from God and every part of Creation is permeated by God's presence. His fairness and compassion is evident in the principles of righteousness, fortune, destiny and cause and effect (Maat, Rennenet, Shai and Meskhenet) which sustain Creation. In order to receive this teaching, she needed to develop faith in her teacher. This enabled her to listen and reflect upon the teaching instead of rejecting the teachings and killing the teacher.

## The Third Parable

The Third Parable has important implications for spiritual life. Hetheru has now turned away from the pit of negativity, the dull state of mind, but she is not free from the delusion of ignorance which is rooted deep within her heart. She still remains in the form of a wildcat and even though she has had certain glimpses of the divine glory of her Higher Self, she is still partially entangled in the lower self as well. This is the predicament of many people. They have some inkling of their higher spiritual essence but they are caught up in the egoism which still remains in the form of ignorance, lower desires and wrong thinking. It must be cleansed from their minds. This state is known as *agitation of mind.* It is characterized by impure thoughts and feelings based on ignorance of the higher spiritual reality, and on indulgence in egoistic feelings, selfishness and individuality. When the mind is agitated it cannot understand or feel clearly. The thoughts and feelings are tainted with illusion and desire. This is why, when strong emotions and feelings take control of the mind, the mind cannot reason objectively. Likewise, when people are deeply involved in worldly activities with an egoistic intent, they are actually moving away from self-discovery and intensifying the illusions, distractions, and worldly desires in their minds. It is like going to the beach and staying at the surface, being aware only of the waves, and never going down below the surface to experience the peace, calm and homogenous equanimity below. Conversely, when a person lives in accordance with the teaching and affirms the spiritual reality in all areas of life, working to promote harmony, peace and truth in their life, they are moving closer to self-discovery. They may have an active life and still experience inner peace and the divine presence. This is the ideal.

## Control of the Mind

The Goal of Sema Tawy Uaah [Egyptian Yoga of Meditation] is to
Calm the movements of the Mind.
If the mind is Calmed a person can discover the Soul.
So the process means controlling:
*Thoughts, Feelings, Actions and Desires*

# IMPORTANT: There are two main forms of Meditative practice:

## Two-Fold Method of Controlling the Mind

| Formal Meditation | Informal Meditation |
| --- | --- |
| Posture – Stationary<br>Chanting<br>Breathing Exercises<br>Concentration Exercises | Imhotep – Peacefulness<br>Righteousness<br>Detatchment – Dispassion<br>Moderation – Balance in All Actions |

## Meditation Leads to Cessation of Identification With the Mind and Movements

## Methods to Control the Mind (Integral Sema {Yoga})

-Through Understanding (Wisdom)*
-Through Resolving Emotions*
-Through Right Action (Maat Philosophy)*
-Through Meditation (Transcending Thought)*

*All methods lead to Control of the Life Force energy or Serpent Power which moves in the mind.

## Essential Mental Disciplines (Goals of Sema {Yoga})

Dispassion
Detatchment
Intellectual Understanding (Faith)
Intuitional Understanding (Experience)
Serenity of Mind (Inner Peace)
Strong Will (Spiritual Strength)

When the mind is calm it can see the truth clearly and one's ideas about oneself also become clear as well. A person may feel great in the morning, full of anticipation and cheerfulness because they believe they will make money that day. So the mind is agitated with the expectation of making money and the myriad of things they will do with it. They are not thinking about the possibility of not getting what they want. This person has deluded himself or herself into expecting a desire to be fulfilled. In the afternoon the expectation is not met so the frustration sets in and depression ensues. They become angry and belligerent because they have attached themselves to the roller coaster of emotions and egoistic expectation based on the activities they perform in the world of human experience. They are detached from the world of the spirit, so they have no awareness of the higher reality. They are like a boat caught up in a storm, going up with elation and down with depression, with no end in sight. They miss out on the more profound positive feeling which lies below the waves of elation and depression. When one steadies the mind, not allowing it to become dejected (to the capacity that one can do so) or elated (again to one;s capacity), one experiences a greater degree of the depths of one's true being. This is the practice of keeping the scales of Maat balanced. In this steadiness of mind they will experience an expansion in consciousness and enjoy a more profound experience of happiness, called bliss, and peace, called hetep. The bliss and peace of this expansion in consciousness is experienced in greater and greater degrees by an initiate or aspirant who practices keeping the mind calm at all times. It is really what people are trying acquire by continuously trying to arrange situations which will make they feel good (elated) and escape from situations which make them feel bad (dejection, depression). However, because they settle either for elation if they can arrange the situation or dejection if they cannot (both of which cause mental agitation), they never get to experience that which they are really seeking, true abiding happiness (*awet ab* - bliss) and peace of mind (*hetep*). The experience of the temporary happiness which is termed elation is like one drop of water in the ocean as compared to the whole ocean which is experienced when the mind attains the state of perfect serenity and enlightenment dawns on that individual. So the masses of people, feeling that by pursuing the sensual pleasures of life they are being good to themselves, are in reality short changing themselves. They are being miserly with themselves, settling for so little, when in fact with a little discipline and self-effort they can have so much. Agitation arises from desires. Desires exist in the mind because it is searching to fulfil a deep longing for wholeness. The mind is erroneously operating based on the concept that acquiring something, entering into a relationship with someone or experiencing some kind of pleasure will fulfill the need, but all activities in the relative world cannot satisfy the need because all activities there are transitory and the mind itself is transitory. It is not possible to experience abiding peace, happiness and joy with something that is transitory, unpredictable and impermanent (ever-changing).

A spiritual aspirant learns to understand the hollowness* of emotions and the futility of worry, pleasure-seeking, wealth, fame and sentimental egoistic values of society and popular culture. A spiritual aspirant is not caught up in them nor does an aspirant indulge in expectations and desires based on illusion. Instead an aspirant pursues reason and truth. Impure thoughts may not necessarily be evil thoughts. They can be based on ignorance alone even if their outcome appears to be evil. The root cause of impurity in the mind is ignorance of the Higher Self. Examples of impure thoughts may be, "I am alone in this world and nobody cares for me," or "I am a miserable human being and there may be a God but he does not care for me," or "life is for pleasure and I will get mine any way I can and I don't care about anyone else," or "life has no purpose so I don't care whether I live or die." *(void, desolation, emptiness.)

A spiritual aspirant must learn to think positively, keep the mind steady in pleasure and pain by surrendering when one's expectations are not met and have positive expectations and desires. These will lead to freedom from negativity and ultimately to the experience of enlightenment. A positive desire is to desire to become pure of heart and a positive expectation is to look forward to the experience of discovering God. These are in accord with the teachings and serve to fulfill the purpose (goal) of human life. Other examples of positive desires are desires to help humanity and nature, visit spiritual centers or read spiritual texts.

The spiritual teaching shows the fallacy of ignorant and egoistic thinking and the manner in which it degrades the mind to the extent of causing people to act callously and selfishly. When a person acts in negative ways he or she is in reality going against the inner nature, the higher truth deep down. This acts as a poison in one's mind and body which manifests as physical or mental diseases such as agitation, restlessness, arguing nature, selfishness, etc. When the problem becomes acute, advanced mental and physical diseases arise such as schizophrenia, dementia, delusions, hallucinations, ulcers, cancers, etc. Ultimately, the affliction of negativity in the mind leads to the disease of negative karma, hellish conditions and reincarnation.

So Djehuty tells Hetheru the parable of the two jackals who were spared by the lion because of their *calmness and truthfulness*. As previously discussed, calmness is an important quality for a spiritual aspirant. It implies remaining balanced in the time when there is temptation or when there is disturbance in the environment. It means maintaining an equal vision towards all things and not letting one's emotions hold sway when a decision needs to be made. It

89

means controlling the emotions and desires and not allowing them to control one's life. It means living in accordance with truth and reason and holding fast to correct action even when the mind and body desires something else. In Ancient Egyptian Maat Philosophy,* this practice is referred to as "keeping the balance." Calmness of mind implies developing equal vision or impartiality. This means not being affected by the ever-changing situations and circumstances of life, be they positive or negative. It means cultivating positive desires and then remaining centered in one's own self, neither expecting fulfillment of desires nor expecting that they will not be fulfilled, but surrendering to the divine will who knows what is best. It is the art of remaining neutral in all conditions and knowing that the Divine will provide the appropriate result for all actions performed. This discipline also involves drawing inner satisfaction from a job well done and allowing the Divine to flow through you for the betterment of all humanity instead of looking to fulfil a personal desire or receive a fruit or reward for what you have done. The discipline of calmness means remaining balanced when things are going well, and also when they do not seem to be going well, knowing that God has everything well in hand and that whatever the outcome may be, you will never lose God, eternity and immortality. It is understanding that even if the Divine Self brings you some situation that appears to be negative, that it is ultimately for your greater benefit and spiritual enlightenment. A person who has advanced in calming the mind can experience oneness with God, the source of peace and bliss, at any time and in any place.  *See the book *Introduction to Maat Philosophy* by Dr. Muata Ashby.

Truthfulness is important because life is meaningless without it. Without truth, nothing real can be known. If a person lives their life in accordance with ignorance and egoism, everything they experience will be an illusion. Consequently they will never be able to discover true happiness and inner peace. For example, most people believe that if they win a lottery they will be happy. This is an ignorant understanding. Their wealth gained from the lottery will only lead to more mental agitation (elation, greed) and frustrations later on; an exsacerbation of their present psychological characteristics and tendencies. They will only be happy for a short period of time, because even one lifetime is short as compared to eternity. In addition, they are creating false impressions in their unconscious as to the source of true happiness. Consequently, in their future lifetimes, they will be very unhappy whenever they find themselves without lots of money. It is so important that an aspirant make every effort to understand that the only source of happiness is the Spirit which you are, which has manifested through theconditoining of your own *ariu* that has been processed through *Meskhenet*.  And even when your spiritual aspiration is not strong enough to prevent you from deluding yourself and you find yourself elated as a result of having acquired some object or situation in the world of time and space, remind yourself that the source of that happiness you are experiencing is due to the Self, and not the object. Also reflect on the spiritual teachings which tells you that the happiness which you experience as a result of some happening in the world is like one drop as compared to the ocean of happiness that awaits you when you attain Enlightenment. Then and only then will you discover true happiness and true wealth. The happiness that objects and situations offer is like a mirage. No sooner do you attain it and experience it for a short time than it just vanishes into thin air, leaving you feeling insecure and miserable. You must continuously reflect that true happiness comes from discovering the Higher Self who is infinite peace, immortal, eternal and has the power to overcome all obstacles.

## The Fourth Parable

The Fourth Parable relates to **humility**. Humility is a quality that should not be confused with humiliation. It is an advanced quality which allows a person to rise above the lower self by sublimating the negative aspects of the ego. Think about it. You may know people or may even recognize yourself acting in egoistic ways based on pride in your own physical prowess, strength, beauty, possessions, fame, etc. These egoistic patterns have been developed as you grew up in society and accepted its values which emphasize physical beauty, sexuality, fame, wealth and so on. But if these values are correct, why is it that the people who have the most money, fame, opportunity for sex relations, plastic surgery and notoriety in the world are not the happiest people in the world? Why is it that they are susceptible to the same failings, misfortunes and calamities as all other people? There is a great illusion in popular society that most people follow without examining closely, that there is some situation, possession or person in the world that can bring them happiness. People have been searching for such an object since the beginning of time, without any success. Hetheru had searched for it in vain. Now she realized that what she was searching for was something she already had within herself. No person or living creature can escape *Meskhenet* or the jaws of death. This must be clearly understood.

Your ego is not a real part of your personality. It is an illusion which you are sustaining due to an error in understanding your true Higher Self. Your ego, meaning your personality, sense organs, physical body and thoughts are in reality transient aspects of yourself. They are instruments that the soul uses in order to have experiences in the world of time and space. They are not absolute realities. This is why at the time of death, the unenlightened soul sheds the personality and ego and moves on to other experiences. It will reincarnate at some point in the future and use a new ego personality, just as a person may change clothing. When you act in accordance with righteousness you are also putting down the ego. When the ego is not given prominence in the personality it becomes an instrument instead of an obstruction. It becomes a servant instead of a slave master who forces a person to enter into situations and entanglements which at the beginning seem to promise happiness, but which later will lead to great pain and sorrow.

When a person overlooks performing correct action in favor of indulging in the personal desires, their actions will be based on egoism. All actions tainted with egoism will inevitably lead to disappointment and frustration at some point in the future. Therefore, the inability to act in accordance with truth must be understood as a defect in the personality, a mental illness. It is the illness of **delusion**. Delusion is intensified by activities which bolster the ego, spiritual ignorance and the egoistic desires. So the pleasure-seeking mentality, the pursuit of sensual pleasures, the desire to possess objects, wealth, fame and power for personal aggrandizement are all examples of egoistic desires which lead to delusion and mental agitation.

The spiritual teaching allows a person to discover a higher form of fulfillment. It allows a person to understand the underlying basis of Creation, and the illusoriness of desiring fleeting egoistic pursuits and perishable objects. You need to have some relationships and possessions in the course of a normal life. However, you should never hold onto anything in the world even as you are experiencing it and possessing it. Your possessions and relationships should be based on righteousness and truth, and never on ostentatiousness, greed and lust.

The spiritual lifestyle allows a spiritual aspirant to go beyond the erroneous desires, thoughts and feelings that cause agitation of the mind. It shows a person how to calm the mind. When the mind is calmed it becomes clear just as a lake becomes clear when the waves subside. This calmness or serenity of mind allows the real essence of a person to become visible and the ego becomes transparent. When the mind is cleansed, the Divine Self comes into clear view as the reality sustaining the ego. When the mind is purified, devoid of the pressure of desires and illusions, one reaches a state of harmony with the universe. This state of consciousness which a person experiences when the mind is serene is referred to as *lucidity of mind.* Lucidity is the quality which is characterized by detachment from the ego and identification with the Higher Self, God. Therefore, lucidity of mind is the objective of all spiritual disciplines because it leads to spiritual enlightenment (self-knowledge) and freedom from ignorance, egoism and negative karma. A person who is lucid is free from attachments and internally fulfilled. He or she expresses goodwill towards all and displays a *gentle nature*. This was Hetheru's condition when she entered the city of Waset.

It is notable that Hetheru was a vicious beast when she was in the states of dullness and agitation, but then she reverted back to her true form when she became gentle, kind and calm. This points to the fact that the source of ugliness and negativity within the human personality lies in the state of mind which a person adopts. The mindset which a person adopts is in accordance with their level of spiritual evolution. Therefore, ignorance and delusion lead to ugliness and negativity in the form of anger, hatred, greed, selfishness, jealousy, conflict, frustration and violence. On the other hand, serenity and lucidity of mind lead to the expression of peace, gentleness, compassion, love and other virtuous qualities in one's personality.

*Detachment* from the ego should not be a hard concept to understand. Most people's concept of self is based on their identification with the ego. This is because the ego and its desires, longings and beliefs are all that the person understands. However, spiritual practice allows a person to discover the underlying essence of the mind. This occurs to every person in the world every single day of their lives, albeit indirectly. When you go to sleep you experience dreams but at other times there are no dreams and no awareness of the world. What happened to your ego? It dissolved into your consciousness just as a wave subsides into the ocean from which it arises. When you wake up you feel refreshed. You experience a transcendental feeling, but do not specifically remember what happened. What would happen if you were to cause the waves of thoughts and egoistic desires to subside while you were in the state of wakefulness? You would discover, in a conscious way, the same truth that you experience in deep dreamless sleep. You would discover that there is a deeper part of yourself which sustains your personality and day to day realities. It is this deeper essence of who you are that manifests as the three states of consciousness (dullness, agitation and lucidity) and the seven manifestations of psycho-spiritual consciousness (energy centers). This is your Higher Self, that part of you which is not dependent on the world and the desires of the ego. When you discover and abide in this state of consciousness you are freed from the lower states. You become an enlightened Sage, a knower of the true meaning of the teachings and the monarch or ruler over every aspect of your personality. You become supremely peaceful, *hetep,* and you rise above all temptations and all illusions. The Higher Self is to be discovered by the following plan as presented in the story of Hetheru and Djehuty. They have been discussed at length throughout this gloss and are presented summarily below. Even though the principles from *The Story of Hetheru and Djehuty* have been presented below as a succession in a hierarchical order, all of these disciplines are best practiced in an integral fashion. This means that you do not wait to perfect Maat before starting to practice detachment. You should practice all of these as life presents you with opportunities to test your spiritual strength or Hetheru faculty.

94

# THE PATH TO SPIRITUAL ENLIGHTENMENT

⬆

### Detachment

⬆

### Humility

⬆

### Calmness, Truthfulness and Gentleness

⬆

### Devotion To The Divine

⬆

### Wisdom: Listening, Reflection and Meditation

⬆

### Reverence and respect for the Spiritual Teacher

⬆

### Preceptorship - Association with an authentic Spiritual Teacher

⬆

### Practice Maat and live in accordance with the Principle of Meskhenet

⬆

### Spiritual Ignorance: Dullness and Agitation

An ordinary person needs to enjoy the company of another person or experience some situation in time and space to feel joy and happiness. This is the difference between an un-enlightened person and a person who is advancing spiritually. A person who has experienced the absolute state of consciousness can remember the experience and feel unobstructed bliss and joy. This act of recalling the experience of the Divine is known as remembrance of God. When the feeling of oneness with the Divine becomes a perpetual experience, that state is referred to as spiritual enlightenment or achieving oneness with the Divine. Ordinary people experience tiny and transient glimpses of this bliss and joy in daily life as happiness and elation. However, they ascribe it to some object they acquired, some person in their life or some situation they saw as beneficial. Others experience joy spontaneously for no apparent reason, but it fades away as mysteriously as it came. A Sage (practitioner of Sema {Yoga}) learns to discover the source of bliss and unobstructed joy and to abide there continuously by not allowing egoistic desires, expectations, sentimentality, anger, hatred, greed, etc. to cloud their experience. The unobstructed experience of joy and peace is what all living things are striving for in various ways, even if they do not realize it. Therefore, it is said that an enlightened Sage has accomplished the most important task in life, achieving which, nothing is left to be achieve. Therefore, they direct their energy to the spiritual upliftment of humanity.

The character of Djehuty and his relationship to Hetheru implies another important teaching in relation to the teacher-student relationship. An advanced spiritual teacher does not see him or herself as the originator of the teaching. It is God who is working through them to bring the teaching forth for the benefit of all humanity. People often ask where God is when bad things are happening and why there is no one to help in time of need. People need to understand that God is everywhere, especially in the heart of authentic spiritual preceptors and in the good intentions of others. However, people need to purify their hearts, because an impure heart that is constantly producing negative thoughts and feelings will not be able to recognize an authentic spiritual preceptor or the good intentions of others. Such a mind will become like poison, killing the vision of goodness in life. Consequently, such dull personalities will constantly lead themselves into negative situations and relationships. Thus, their negative mind set and actions will lead them to experiences which seemingly reinforce their own erroneous beliefs. They would not benefit from the teachings of even the greatest spiritual teachers such as Djehuty, Aset, Jesus, Buddha, etc. Such personalities will have to go through many incarnations where they will eventually learn to follow the precepts of Maat. Therefore, the compassion of the Goddess is so great that she has come to the world in the form of the scriptural writings, compassion and the spirit of service in the human heart, Sages, Saints and the high mystical philosophy and religious iconography.

There is also a mystical significance to the rejoicing in the cities when Hetheru returned to her rightful place. The cities mentioned, Anu, Het-ku-Ptah and Waset, relate to cities of the gods of the great Ancient Egyptian Trinity of *Amun-Ra-Ptah*. The Ancient Egyptian Hymns of Amun contain the key to understanding the mystical meaning of the teaching. The Ancient Egyptian teaching "Neberdjer-Amun-Ra-Ptah" is explained as follows. Neberdjer means the "Supreme Being." Amun-Ra-Ptah represent the triune manner in which the Supreme Being manifests Creation. Amun represents witnessing consciousness or self-awareness. Ra represents the cosmic mind which sustains all mental activity and is the means for consciousness to interact with Creation, the light or power of consciousness. Ptah represents the physical universe with which the witnessing consciousness interacts. This triad is also related to human life. All human beings have three bodies, the physical, astral and causal. The soul in every human being is like a spark of the Self, Neberdjer, who uses these bodies in order to have experiences in the varied forms of life in Creation.

The Trinity also relates to the human mind. The mind of a human being experiences three states of awareness, waking, dream and dreamless sleep, as well as three modes of manifestation, "dullness, agitation and lucidity." Thus, the return of Hetheru signifies the rejoicing in all aspects of a person's personality, the emotions, intellect, will and physical nature. This is, of course, a description of a human being who has attained spiritual perfection.

The seven day festivity relates to the seven centers of psycho-spiritual consciousness. Hetheru is the goddess of the seven aspects of consciousness in her form as the seven divine Hetheru cows. The one Supreme Being in the form of a bull (Asar-Osiris), expresses in seven modes of consciousness (the seven cows). This expression of the spirit is symbolized by Hetheru in her seven aspects. Hetheru represents divine consciousness emanating from the Divine Self (Eye of Ra emanating from the Sun). She (divine consciousness) expresses herself (itself) as the essence which sustains the mind of every human being as well. Every human being has seven psycho-spiritual consciousness centers in their astral body. These act as transducers of psychic energy from the soul level of consciousness. They sustain the physical body. Each center relates to an aspect of human personality. As a person develops, the *Arat* or the Serpent Power energy (Inner Life Force known as Kundalini in India or Chi in China) of the goddess, these energy centers are cleansed and their power is allowed to unfold. Thus, a human being evolves spiritually through the power of the goddess. The Serpent Power automatically awakens when a person studies and practices the teachings. However, the process of raising one's spiritual power may be aided by specific exercises such as concentration, proper breathing, righteous action, devotion to the Divine, meditation on the meanings of the spiritual symbols and surrendering to the will of the Higher Self (God). These techniques allow a person to transform their waking personality so that they may discover their innermost Self: God. For more on the Serpent Power and the techniques for cultivating it see the book "The Serpent Power" by Dr. Muata Ashby.

# The Three States of Consciousness

## THE EYE AS A METAPHOR

The Eye coming into physical form as the lynx or lioness is a symbol of human existence. It represents the human soul. In the same way that the Eye is a "ray" or "projection" of Ra, the Supreme Being, the human soul is a ray or projection of the Supreme Being. Thus, the plight of the Eye is a parable which the Sages of Ancient Egypt composed in order to explain human existence and to impart the knowledge of spiritual enlightenment for spiritual aspirants. In this context it is similar in most respects to other initiatic scriptures, especially those from India (The Upanishads, Bhagavad Gita, Yoga Vasistha).

The teachings are given through three main characters in the story. These are *Ra, Hetheru* and *Djehuty*. Hetheru displays three distinct states of consciousness throughout the myth. In so doing the myth outlines the three important states of religion and religious practice in a highly artistic and entertaining manner. True religious practice is made up of three stages of spiritual practice as previously discussed. Therefore, it requires three stages of teaching or initiatic education. The first stage is composed of the events of the myth. This includes the events of the story, the characters and/or deities within the story, the plot and basic themes within the story. The second stage is the Ritual. Ritual includes the observances, ceremonies, customs, etc., related to the myth. The third level of religion is the Mystical Experience. This third level is the true objective of all religious practices. Without this stage, religion becomes dry and ineffective. When people only practice the first and second levels of religion the practice often becomes personal and egoistic as well as dogmatic and subjective. This is the breeding ground for conflict between religions as well as misunderstanding about what true religious practice is all about.

## *The Mystical Experience: Pure Consciousness*

In the beginning Hetheru is one with Ra. She experiences awareness of her essential nature as being united with the Supreme. This is the mystical experience. The mystical experience is the true state of being. It represents a full awareness of the spiritual Self as well as an awareness of the unity of everything in creation. This is the true state of human consciousness. This state of consciousness is characterized by all-pervasiveness, infinite expansion, infinite freedom, infinite awareness and infinite peace. In Indian mysticism the states of consciousness are called *"Gunas"* or modes of expression in which consciousness (God) expresses. In Ancient Egyptian wisdom it is recognized that there are mixed personalities in the world and even among aspirants. People who act righteously sometimes and at others not, are explained in the understanding gained from the myth of Hetheru and

Djehuti, of the three forms of human personalities, ⲣⲉⲣ *beq*-"Lucid, to be bright to see," ⲛⲉϣ *Neshsh* –"agitated, disturbed- bothered, distracted" and ⲩⲙⲉⲧ *umet-ab* - "dull, dense, dull of heart." The lucid personality is content and well adjusted, a seeker of higher culture and an experienced of inner peace and spiritual upliftment. The agitated personality is constantly swinging from peaceful to non-peaceful thoughts and actions, seeking for fulfillment and sometimes finding temporary happiness and when that wears off then need to search again. This search sometimes leaves them elated and at other times depressed. Sometimes there are lucid glimpses of the higher perspective in life and then these are shut off due to ignorance, and desires that cause mental distractions and passions that cloud the intellect. The dull personality is incapable of envisioning the higher perspective of life. It seeks for what is base and degraded as it is. The intellect of such a person is atrophied. In a higher, more advanced sense there are only two groups, the

*Nehastu* 𓏠𓅱𓂋𓁹𓀀 -"spiritually awakened" and the 𓏠𓅽𓏤 {ignorant} "worldly".

## The Distracted State (Agitation)

When she (Hetheru) was sent (projected) into time and space (the phenomenal world) to perform a task in the service of the Divine (Ra) she fell prey to individual conscience and egoistic desire. In particular she becomes filled with anger and develops a need to satisfy her desire for flesh and blood. This is a state in which she became forgetful of her original condition. This lower state of being is a condition wherein the soul is overpowered with delusion due to the overwhelming pressure of desires, thoughts and strong emotions. These act as clouds which block the human personality from having a clear vision of the Self. They are called fetters and anyone who is fettered is known as one who is in the state of bondage. This state of mind is characterized by restlessness, distraction, dissatisfaction, lack of fulfillment, constant movement, etc. In relation to the Gunas of Indian mysticism, this state of consciousness is known as *Rajas*.

The human soul uses the mind and senses in order to have human experiences in much the same way as a person uses glasses to see the world. When the glasses are colored, anything that is seen through them is colored. In the same way when the soul uses the mind and senses to "know," everything that is known in this manner is "colored" by the thoughts, feelings, sentiments, egoism, etc. Therefore, the mind that is beset with ignorance, anger, hatred, anxiety, delusion, etc. will act as a veil which blocks the vision of the innermost Self. This state is represented by Hetheru as she runs through the land seeking to satisfy her endless desire to slay and consume human beings. The desires in a mind that is constantly assaulted by the fetters are endless. No sooner does one desire become fulfilled before another arises. This is because ignorance is feeding on ignorance, and ignorance can never satiate ignorance. Hetheru in the state of delusion believes that she must continue to search out, kill and eat flesh and blood in order to satisfy her innermost urge. Since the desire is of the flesh (her body, mind and ego), it is never possible to satisfy it. As long as she continues to believe that this is her true desire and purpose she will continue in an endless search for fulfillment in this manner. This state of consciousness is characterized by a constriction in consciousness. No longer is there all-pervasiveness or peace but a squeezing pressure of desires.

"The Body belongs to the Earth,
Soul belongs to Heaven"

—Ancient Egyptian Proverb

This is the miserable predicament of human embodiment. When the human soul becomes embodied (associated with a human form-the body, mind and senses) the pressure of these (body, mind and senses) cause the soul to forget its true nature. It begins to believe that it is the body and that the feelings, sentiments, desires of the mind, senses and body are its own. This form of delusion leads people on an endless search through life trying to satisfy their need for companionship, comfort, happiness, etc., through worldly objects and other human personalities. However, the real need and innermost desire is to discover the Self, to know "Who am I".

In this state most people are concerned with getting rich or acquiring objects which they perceive as sources of pleasure. There is little thought given to why there is only a brief period of apparent fulfillment once an object or situation that was desired is finally acquired or achieved. There is only the thought: Somewhere in this world there is a situation or some thing which will make me supremely happy and which will fulfill my desires. However this "something" is never to be found in the world of time and space.

"Searching for one's self in the world is the pursuit of an illusion."

—Ancient Egyptian Proverb

People in the *Distracted State* are considered as "normal" by mainstream society. People in this state will often act out of selfishness and will not consider the consequences of their actions. They experience a *Thermometer Existence.* This means that they experience mood swings and a constant flow of emotions and desires. They may be reasonably honest under ordinary conditions but when under the pressure of temptation they may lie, cheat or steal.

Another characteristic of the *Distracted State* is that people meet in conversations and talk about any and all subjects without coherence, or rationality. For example, two people may meet at lunch time and discuss several subjects from the taste of their sandwich to the breakfast they had that day, to the new movie playing, to the weather forecast, to the latest intrigue of their favorite soap opera star, to the ugly tie of their boss and then go back to their job. The conversation flows from one subject to another without any rhyme or reason and it is all mindless and inane talk. A thoughtful person would not engage in such a confused dialogue. She or he would remain quiet. This would make them seem abnormal to the general population.

You must understand that what the masses consider to be good and normal is in reality abnormal. It is an aberration from the higher reality wherein it is possible to experience inner fulfillment and peace. The distracted manner in which most people carry on is an expression of their feeling of emptiness which must continuously be filled with excitement and action. A person who has experienced inner fulfillment does not require interaction with others for the sake of interaction and does not require action in order to feel as if something fulfilling is "going on" and "I am alive", etc. Such a person who displays calmness, self-sufficiency, mental poise, equanimity, peacefulness and who is not susceptible to stress under stressful conditions is seen as abnormal by a distracted personality. People who do not feel the need to seek excitement through parties, sports, entertainments of various types, overindulging in food, sex or drink, etc. are seen as social bores by the masses, and yet this advanced state of being is the real evidence of psycho-spiritual advancement in life.

There are many intellectuals in all fields, including spirituality, who engage in debates and intellectual discussions for the sake of argument. Logic is not studied for a higher purpose but for the sake of logic itself. Under these conditions the mind can construct any form of reasoning which will support its viewpoint.

The power of reasoning and speech is of paramount importance because what you understand is what determines your experiences in the outer world as well as in the inner. Your speech is an expression of your innermost beliefs and ideals, your consciousness. Therefore, you should not allow your intellectual capacity to become retarded, melancholic, gloomy, dejected or spiritless. Intellectualism with no higher, sublime purpose eventually leads to dullness. The proof of this is the long history of intellectuals who have committed crimes and created the most anti-humane forms of philosophy throughout the world. Two examples of this are the African Slave Trade and the racism of Nazi Germany, both of which were supported by many intellectuals of the time. Even today there are those who create elaborate treatises which seek to prove the superiority of one group over another based on sex, economics, genetics, etc. All of these criteria are relative and illusory. Therefore, anyone who engages in such intellectual activity is to be considered as being equally caught in the ignorance of egoism as a backward person who never went to school even for a day and who has not learnt to interact with people of other groups. Thus, intellectual persons, even those who may seem cultured and sophisticated, cannot automatically be considered more advanced than an illiterate person.

## The State of Dullness

When Hetheru is given the drugged beer she was immersed in a state of consciousness characterized by a deep stupor. This is a state of mind wherein there is such degradation that the personality expresses ignorance, negativity, animosity, grief, hatred, etc. which had previously been in a dormant state. Ra decreed that she should be given the potion because she was so deluded that she would not respond to any form of persuasion based on reason or relation of kinship. Have you ever tried to reason with a person who is in the throes of passion or anger? Have you tried to control yourself when in this state? In the *Distracted State*, the mind is clouded and the intellect or reasoning ability is weakened. People often fall in with bad company and are influenced by peer pressure. In the *Dullness State* the delusion has deepened so far that there is a lashing out, a desire for destruction of the environment as well as self-destruction. Hetheru has reached a state in which she will destroy anything which lies in her path. Thus, this state implies intensified anger and hatred as well as laziness, sleepiness, inertness, idleness, indolence, shiftlessness, slothfulness and sluggishness.

When consciousness sinks into deep dullness people may commit murder and/or enter into conflicts which could be life-threatening because they are compelled by their emotions and desires. They will consume substances which are poisonous such as cigarettes, drugs, or meat, even though they may find out that these substances are destroying their body and mind. They will indulge in sensual pleasures (anything that gives physical pleasure) and will become extremely angry if anything comes in the way of their satisfying their perceived desires. They will become violent with the slightest provocation. Sometimes the movement toward destruction is directed inward. This leads to self-inflicted injuries, insipidity, lassitude and deep depression.

When the degradation becomes severe people can commit the most heinous acts of violence and crimes of the most extreme, shocking and reprehensible nature. Others may become incapacitated due to inner negativity to such a degree that they can no longer sustain the practical realities of life. This leads to insanity, homelessness, suicide, etc. In Indian mysticism this state of consciousness is called *"Tamas"*.

## The State of Lucidity (Harmony, Purity and Balance)

(26) "I HAVE NOT STOPPED MY EARS AGAINST THE WORDS OF RIGHT AND WRONG."

—From The Ancient Egyptian
Book of Coming Forth By Day

When Hetheru met with Djehuty a new form of awareness began to develop in her heart. At first she desired to kill and eat him, however, his beguiling charm and eloquence caught her interest. She spared his life and began to listen to him. In so doing she was opening the door to expansion in consciousness.

Most human beings are caught between the first two stages of consciousness at one time or another. There is a mixture of distraction, movement and dullness. In this state a human being does not want to sit still in order to listen to spiritual discourses about the nature of the soul and about the method to attain spiritual enlightenment, and if forced to do so, the mind falls into a state of dullness and she/he feels asleep (a state of extreme dullness).

It is only the stress of egoistic desires which is suppressing that which is positive, true and good within the human heart. In some brief and rare occasions there is an experience of peace, balance, contentment and tranquility. Many times these feelings are experienced for a brief period of time after an object of desire is acquired or a situation which one desired comes true. These experiences are only glimpses of the totality of happiness and peace which is in the heart. However, in order to discover this, the body, mind and senses must reach a state of balance, harmony and peace. This is possible though the practices of Sema {Yoga} (Listening, Reflecting upon, Living in accordance* with and Meditating upon the teachings). *(practicing the teachings of MAAT)

When Yoga is practiced a purifying movement wherein the ignorance, delusion, restlessness, anger, anxiety, hatred, greed, lust, egoism, selfishness, and vices such as pride, covetousness, lust, anger, envy, gluttony, and sloth within the heart are cleansed. Therefore, Djehuty represents the light of reasoning and intuitional understanding about the innermost reality within the heart. Djehuty is the Sage who is sent by God to find the wayward child (the soul) to impart wisdom which leads to illumination of the heart and inner discovery of the truth. This principle is so pervasive in human culture that it has found expression in the Initiatic Way of Education as practiced first in

103

ancient times in the Ancient Egyptian Temples, and later in the Indian Upanishads and epic myths of Krishna and Rama, and much later in the Christian baptism of Jesus by John the Baptist. These stories have one factor in common. It is the relationship of the Sage with the disciple wherein spiritual knowledge is imparted.

The myth of Hetheru and Djehuty is similar to the other important Initiatic myth of Ancient Egypt, *The Asarian Resurrection* in which the young child Heru is taught about the mysteries of the soul and the universe by his mother and Spiritual Preceptor (teacher) Isis. In modern times this tradition of the *Spiritual Preceptor-Aspirant relationship* has been continued through the Gurus of Indian Yoga and the Sufi Gurus of the Near East and in Egypt. In popular culture this teaching has found expression through popular theater such as *Hamlet,* and in films such as *The Star Wars Trilogy* and *The Lion King.* (see the Book *Initiation Into Egyptian Yoga* by Muata Ashby)

However, before spiritual knowledge can be imparted the spiritual aspirant must have aspiration. This implies a desire to go beyond the pettiness and sorrow of ordinary human existence as well as the maturity to accept responsibility for one's condition. This means that there can be no blaming of others for one's troubles. It is one's own Karma which has led one to one's present conditions, good or bad. Conversely, it is one's present self-effort in the area of *Sheti* (spiritual practice) which can lead one out of adversity and into spiritual as well as material prosperity.

Lucidity implies reason, clarity, wit, sanity, soundness, saneness. Also it implies righteousness, truthfulness, universal love, harmony, peace and selflessness. Therefore, in order to develop lucidity, a spiritual aspirant needs to practice these virtues in everyday life while at the same time studying the teachings at the feet of authentic Spiritual Preceptors (Sages and Saints). When a positive spiritual movement is engendered there is greater and greater awareness of the deeper spiritual reality culminating is self-discovery. This is symbolized by Hetheru's discovery of her true essential nature as one with Ra, the Supreme Being, and thus assuming her rightful place. Most human beings think their rightful place is as a member of some social, ethnic or political group, etc. In reality this is only an evanescent and minuscule expression of the totality of who they really are. It is like the sun expressing as a reflection in a pool of water falling into a delusion and thinking "I am this little reflection" and forgetting its true identity. So too every human being has forgotten his/her true identity. However, through the compassion and love of the Self (God), the message of truth which leads to spiritual enlightenment, a return home as it were, is brought by the genuine spiritual personalities who have emerged as great teachers throughout history. Their spiritual enlightenment (contact with the Self) allows them to transmit the teachings of the Self for all who wish to find true peace and happiness. Thus, their discourses and writings on the Self (spiritual scripture) are to be considered as authoritative sources for spiritual enlightenment and should be sought after and studied.

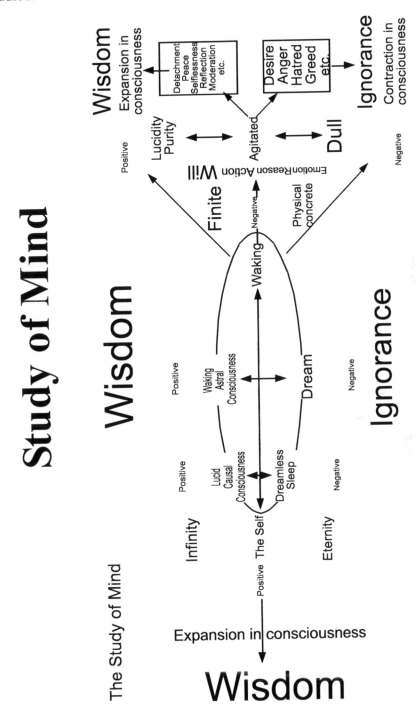

Transcendental Awareness

↑

Lucidity

↑

Distraction

↑

Dullness

   This hekau (Ancient Egyptian utterance, verse or spiritual scripture) contains a profound teaching of mystical spirituality. It comes from a text in which an Ancient Egyptian Sage (Merikare) is teaching about the agitated state of mind by discussing the motivations and causes for the negativity of the "Asiatics" who were constantly attacking Egypt during that time and for several thousands of years before. It teaches the need to maintain equal vision or equanimity of mind. Since material wealth is transient and illusory as we discussed in the last passage, a person cannot be judged by his or her material condition. Rather, a person should be judged by their actions and abilities. Since every human being is innately a divine, immortal Soul, their potential is limitless. What holds people back is their ignorant understanding of life and egoistic feelings which lead to sinful behaviors (behaviors based on vices). If you judge others based on their level of material wealth you are engaging in sin because you are seeing them through your egoistic vision of what is true and real based on ignorance. Virtue is the only true wealth and it expresses in the form of compassion, non-violence, truth, universal love, harmony, sharing, etc. Virtue is an expression of one's understanding of the interconnectedness of life and one's own transcendental existence which is connected to the Supreme Spirit. To the extent that one is aware of one's own Divine nature, virtue manifests through the human personality. To the extent that one is in ignorance about one's own Divine nature, sinful (vice) behavior based on greed, jealousy, egoistic desires, etc., will manifest.

   There is one more important point to realize about the various states of consciousness. Many people believe that when something which they feel is positive, occurs, then this means happiness, peace and harmony have been achieved. For example, people in general feel that when they experience some situation or acquire some object which brings them joy that this signifies happiness and is the goal of life. Upon reflection, in the light of Yogic Mystical Philosophy, it must be understood that both elation and depression, happiness and anger, etc., are both in reality only two forms of agitation. Elation causes one form of distraction and unrest while anger and negativity also cause a form of distraction and unrest. Dullness is also a form of distraction and unrest. As you study and reflect on the teachings of ancient mystical philosophy it should become increasingly clear to you that what most people consider to be true happiness and peace are in reality sources of

106

agitation, stress and distraction from the real source of peace. This is why in Ancient Egyptian mystical philosophy as well as in the mystical philosophy from India there is an emphasis on the practice of balance (MAAT) as the following Hekau* explain. *(Ancient Egyptian Spiritual Scripture)

Creativity is a factor of harmony and inner peace. When there is a raging storm of emotions, anxiety and tension in the mind the flow of inspiration from the transcendental Self is obstructed. Therefore, to promote creativity it is necessary to harmonize one's life as much as possible so as to come into harmony with the higher Self. All activities should be performed in such a way that promotes peace instead of tension. This way of life allows the Inner Self to guide your inner and outer life. This can be achieved if there is constant surrender of egoistic desire to the Divine Will by permitting yourself to be directed by the teachings of Sema {Yoga}.

The preceding teaching speaks volumes about the nature of agitation. The general message is beware of your environment and beware of your surroundings. Harshness in surroundings and general environment can cause negative stress which could lead to an unsettled mind.

An unsettled mind is difficult to control. A mind that is uncontrollable will have difficulty in concentrating. Poor concentration will not allow for reflection. Reflection is necessary to make sense of one's situation and to gain intellectual understanding. A non-reflective, confused or "wrong thinking" mind will have difficulty meditating. A non- meditating mind will have difficulty in transcending the world of apparent dualities. One will be endlessly pulled into the "world" and the apparent thoughts going on in the mind.

As the mind will be caught up in the endless waves of joys and sorrows, it will be unable to find peace. A mind filled with too much joy or too much sorrow due to its experiences in the world will be equally agitated and one will have difficulty concentrating and calming down. One extreme (ex. Joy) leads to another (ex. Pain).

The concept of the *"Miserable Asiatic"* became known in Egypt as the concept of *"The Land of Heru and the Land of Set"*. Since Set is the god of the desert, the Asiatics, who dwelt in the desert lands (Asia Minor), became identified with Set and therefore, Setian behavior (impulsive, selfish, brute force, etc.). The teaching about the miserable Asiatic is of paramount importance because it provides an understanding of how the human mind becomes degraded and violent. A human being who is not nurtured and who is constantly experiencing stress will develop a distracted, negative character. The pressures due to lack of security, not knowing where the next meal is coming from, how to acquire the secure the needs of life and then how to hold onto them, etc., etc., does not allow the inner peace and expansiveness of the inner self to manifest. All of these worries and anxieties cause

107

a degradation in the human mind wherein the concern is not about working with others but competing with them for food, material wealth, mates, etc. The purpose of human existence is to provide a means for the soul to experience and grow in awareness of itself as being one with Creation. This feeling is blissful, supremely satisfying and universal. When the soul in a human being is not allowed to express itself in this manner, the ego in a human being is in control, and this egoism fosters feelings of personal desire, separation, and animosity to anything which prevents the ego from getting what it wants. This is the source of animosity, enmity, anger, hatred and violence in the human experience. Spiritual practice leads a human being to discover a deeper essence of life. True spiritual understanding allows a person to understand where true happiness and peace are to be found. It shows a person that security cannot be found in the world but in that which sustains it.

The Ancient Egyptian teachings presented above are echoed in the ancient Hindu scripture known as "The Bhagavad Gita" in which Lord Krishna instructs his disciple Arjuna. This particular verse comes from the Chapter on the practice of meditation.

32. O Arjuna! The Yogi who sees the likeness of himself in all and thus maintains equal vision in pleasure and pain, he is considered the highest Yogi.

Arjuna then asked about the way in which the mind can be controlled.

33. Arjuna asked: O Krishna, I do not see how it is possible to maintain the steady state of Yogic equanimity which you have taught. This mind is ever so restless!

34. Verily, O Krishna, the mind is fickle, impetuous and turbulent. To me it seems more difficult to control the mind than it is to control the wind.

35. *Bhagavan (Lord) Krishna said: Indeed the mind is restless and difficult to control, but can be brought under control by the exercise of Abhyasa (repeated effort) and Vairagya (dispassion).*

36. It is my opinion that Yoga is difficult for anyone who is lacking self-control. But it can be attained by one who has mastered his lower self if he adopts the proper means.

These instructions bring out important teachings in reference to understanding and controlling the mind. Many people become discouraged early in their spiritual practice because they do not obtain discernible results within a short time. Sometimes they try many different techniques without giving any one sufficient time to work. In essence it is like digging for water by making a well but without going deep enough. What would happen if a person was to dig a hole, and after one or two feet stop and begin another hole? He or she would not find any water.

In spiritual practice as in any other human endeavor, sustained practice (repeated effort) is a key to success. In spiritual practice every single time you turn your mind towards the Divine you are actually creating a higher mental impression. Eventually, these positive impressions overpower the negative impressions of ignorance, anger, hatred, greed, etc. This occurs even when there is no discernible benefit. Therefore, even though you may not see immediate results you should continue practicing your spiritual discipline regularly and with faith. Also it is important to practice dispassion and detachment from worldly objects and worldly desires. If these points are not practiced along with your formal meditation efforts you will have little success or very slow success in meditation.

## Witnessing Consciousness and Mindfulness in Ancient Egypt

In Ancient Egypt, the level of consciousness known as the mystical experience or cosmic awareness (Spiritual Enlightenment) was also called *Amun*, "the witness" or "watcher". The understanding of the "witnessing consciousness" achieved a high level of expression in the Ancient Egyptian *Hymns of Amun* and in the teaching of the Ancient Egyptian Trinity of Amun-Ra-Ptah. The line below from the *Hymns of Amun* explains the nature of the witnessing consciousness:

"He the One Watcher who neither slumbers nor sleeps."

The Trinity, Neberdjer: Amun-Ra-Ptah of Ancient Egypt refers to the three states of consciousness and that which transcends them. Amun, the Self, is the "hidden" essence of all things. The Sun, Ra, is the radiant and dynamic outward appearance made manifest in the light of cosmic consciousness. In this aspect, Ptah represents the physical world, the solidification of the projection of consciousness (Amun) made manifest. The Triad also has a reference to the states of consciousness in the human being. The Triad refers to the subject or seer, the object or that which is seen and interaction between the two. In all human experience there is a subject-object-interaction relationship occurring all the time. This is true in the waking as well as the dream states. The seer is Amun, that which is seen is Ptah and the interacting medium or sight is represented by Ra. They are in reality projections or emanations of the transcendental underlying consciousness or Neberdjer. The objective of meditation is to dissolve the trinity into its essential unitary consciousness, the Glorious Light of consciousness.

Just as the subject-object-interaction consciousness of a dream is "unreal", the subject-object-interaction consciousness of the waking state is also unreal and illusory. Even though the phenomenal world experienced in the waking state appears to be abiding and solid, modern science has proven that it is not. These new findings of science confirm the teachings of Ancient Egyptian Sema {Yoga} philosophy, Vedanta and Yoga philosophy of India, Buddhism of India and Taoism of China as well as other mystical philosophies from around the world.

# Summary: The Myth of Hetheru and Djehuty and the Three Modes of Nature

| The State of Lucidity (Harmony, Purity and Balance) | The Distracted State (Agitation) | The State of Dullness |
|---|---|---|
| When Hetheru with Djehuty a new form of awareness began to develop in her heart. At first she desired to kill and eat him, however, his beguiling charm and eloquence caught her interest. She spared his life and began to listen to him. In so doing she was opening the door to expansion in consciousness.<br><br>Most human beings are caught between the first two stages of consciousness at one time or another. There is a mixture of distraction, movement and dullness. In this state a human being does not want to sit still in order to listen to spiritual discourses about the nature of the soul and about the method to attain spiritual enlightenment, and if forced to do so, the mind falls into a state of dullness and she/he feels asleep (a state of extreme dullness). | When she (Hetheru) is sent (projected) into time and space (the phenomenal world) to perform a task in the service of the Divine she falls prey to human sentiment. In particular she becomes filled with anger and develops a need to satisfy her desire for flesh and blood. This a state in which she becomes forgetful (distracted) of her original state due to constant action and lack of reflection. It is a condition wherein the soul is overpowered with delusion of individuality and egoism due to the overwhelming pressure of desires, thoughts and strong emotions. These act as clouds which block the human personality from having a clear vision of the Self. They are called fetters and anyone who is fettered is known as one who is in the state of bondage due to ignorance. This state of mind is characterized by restlessness, distraction, dissatisfaction, lack of fulfillment, constant movement, etc. | When Hetheru was uncontrollable and dangerous to all people and all the gods and goddesses she was overcome with dullness. When she was given the drugged beer she was immersed in a state of consciousness characterized by a deep stupor. This dullness is a state of mind wherein there is such degradation that the personality expresses ignorance, negativity, animosity, grief, hatred, etc. which had previously been in a dormant state. Ra decreed that she should be given the potion because she was so deluded that she would not respond to any form of persuasion based on reason or relation of kinship. This is like giving valium to a violent person. Have you ever tried to reason with a person who is in the throes of passion or anger? Have you tried to control yourself when in this state? In the *Dullness State* the delusion brought on by mental agitation has deepened so far that there is a lashing out, a desire for destruction of the environment as well as self-destruction. Thus, this state implies intensified anger and hatred as well as laziness, sleepiness, inertness, idleness, indolence, shiftlessness, slothfulness and sluggishness. |

# Part 3: The Formal Practice of The Glorious Light Meditation

GLORIOUS LIGHT MEDITATION

## *Introduction*

One unique feature of the GLM is that its instruction is meant for the common people and for both sexes, as well as the clergy. So the practice of meditation in Ancient Egypt and its instruction to the masses, and not just to the Priests and Priestesses, can be traced to at least 800 years earlier than a similar instruction in India. The essential instructions given by Sage Seti I are presented below. The following meditation technique is based on the hieroglyphic text popularly known as the "Destruction of Humankind" which more specifically should be referred to as: "Story of Hetheru and Djehuty." It is to be practiced after hearing the story and having studied its teachings.

### *uaa*

# "Meditation"

Meditation can be practiced by many methods. Some people prefer to concentrate on a religious icon or a Divine form while others choose to allow their mind to flow with an unbroken succession of thoughts directed towards the Absolute. In the practice of the Glorious Light Meditation you will follow the guidelines below. By using certain images and icons (concrete form of practice with names and forms) you will gradually lead yourself to an abstract and transcendental form of practice.

If you reflect upon your own situation you must realize that you have three personalities, the waking personality, the dream personality and the dreamless-sleep personality. Philosophically you can now understand that each of these personalities are relative and therefore illusory, otherwise you would remain the same personality as you go into the different states of mind (waking, dream and dreamless-sleep) and you would take with you the same clothing, the same problems, the same memories, the same possessions, etc. Since this does not occur, one must conclude that they are all variable, depending on the concepts, fancies and desires of the mind of the individual. This points to the wisdom that you do not belong to any of the relative states. You are in reality like a traveler who is going to different train stops at the same familiar locations every day. However, you are traveling without any luggage, ticket or control over your destination through worlds that are not abiding. They are only real in a relative sense when you are caught up in them. Understanding this you should now be able to maintain a certain level of detachment and dispassion toward your life just as you become detached from your dream when you wake up, even though it seemed quite real while you were dreaming. The pride, vanity and egoism related to the body, how good or bad it looks, how attractive it is to others, how famous you are, how wealthy your are, etc., must now begin to seem amusing, if not ridiculous. Also, the pressing desires of life, the problems with relationships and the general struggles of life should now be coming into a perspective based on a larger picture wherein they are all viewed as only a small part of who you are essentially. Your attachments and desires are what is holding you tight and fast to the limited waking reality. Therefore, as you loosen the ties of passion and attachment, you will grow in expansion of consciousness.

*MAUI*

"to think, to ponder, to fix attention, concentration"

**Figure 18: A two dimensional schematic drawing of the mystical interpretation of the levels of human consciousness based on the Glorious Light Meditation System of Ancient Egypt.**

The Spirit encompasses Creation. This includes the unconscious, Intellect and conscious mind of every human being. The meditation allows a human being to expand their experience to go beyond the Ego-personality and to discover the greater essence of existence, the fact that there is more than the physical body, the All-encompassing Spirit, the light of Consciousness which permeates all things, is infinite and eternal. This is God, the Glorious Spirit.

This is the transcendental realm which is beyond time and space, the mind and its thoughts and concepts, and physicality. It is a realm wherein there is no thought and no duality. This is the Supreme Abode of the Self and it is the

114

source of all Creation, which itself appears as duality and multiplicity. With this understanding we can gain greater insight into the mind and its movements. Think of the mind and all existence as an ocean. When there is no vibration in the mind, consciousness is pure, without form. This is what the teaching above is referring to as the realm where "the cedar tree existeth not, where the acacia tree does not put forth shoots, and where the ground neither produces grass nor herbs." When consciousness is in the state of movement, vibration (the terms *Tek* vibration or *Neshsh*-agitation are used), then it takes on the various forms of nature. When you think your mind is actually taking on a form. When there is no thought there is no awareness of forms, time and space or duality. This is the objective of the practice of meditation and spiritual discipline, to discover the realm of consciousness, which is beyond the level of ordinary human awareness. Ordinary human awareness, beset with delusion, ignorance, and distraction, becomes caught in the waves of emotion, elation and depression, etc. In the transcendental realm however, it there is an incomparable experience of bliss and peace, which cannot be described; it can only be experienced in order to be understood.

The mind and the mental substance from which thoughts are made are also composed of vibrations. In the realm described above, where Osiris abides, there is no vibration; "nothing happens" from the point of view of a human being because this realm does not exist as a factor of mentation. Think about it. Everything you know or have experienced in your life has been a factor of your thinking process. In fact, without this thinking process the mind cannot function; it will stand still. When the mind operates it vibrates and this vibration stirs up the ocean of consciousness. This stirring or vibratory process is what people perceive as life experiences, sense perceptions, the awareness of the passage of time, the awareness of space between objects and their thoughts. Upon closer reflection you should realize that throughout all of your experiences, being born, growing to adulthood and middle age throughout the entire aging process, you have been the same all the time. It has always been the same "you" but the experiences have been different. The experiences of your waking life are not really different from those of your dreams. They are all just vibrations in the mental pool of water which is a fraction of the vast ocean of consciousness. The ability to control the mind is possible to the extent that there is awareness of one's separation from and control over the ego. The ego itself is like a vibration, a ripple in the vastness of your consciousness. Therefore, by gaining insight into your true identity as the Self you can gain control over every aspect of your personality (mind, body and sense organs).

Upon reflection on the triad of consciousness it becomes clearer and clearer that the ordinary states are relative and transient. Sometimes people have breakthroughs wherein they discern higher forms of intuition and understanding. However, these come as flashes and soon fade. Oftentimes people shrug it off as a coincidence or in fear of going insane or the idea that an "evil spirit" is messing around with their head, they try to deny the occurrence altogether.

In reality, the three states are merely reflections of the positive states. Thus, the dreamless sleep state has its counterpart in the Lucid Causal Consciousness state wherein there are is awareness but no thoughts or desires. The dream state has its counterpart in the Waking (Lucid) Astral Consciousness state. The ordinary waking state has its opposite or positive in the Transcendental Self or enlightened state.

The personality of every human being is somewhat different from every other. However the Sages of Yoga have identified four basic factors which are common to all human personalities. These factors are: Emotion, Reason, Action and Will. Also, the human personality expresses in three basic formats. These are *Dullness, Agitation* and *Lucidity (Harmony and Purity)*. This means that in order for a human being to properly evolve, all aspects of the personality must develop in an integral fashion. Therefore, four major forms of Yoga disciplines have evolved and each is specifically designed to promote a positive movement in one of the areas of personality. The Sema {Yoga} of Devotional Love enhances and harnesses the emotional aspect in a human personality and directs it towards the Higher Self. The Sema {Yoga} of Wisdom enhances and harnesses the reasoning aspect in a human personality and directs it towards the Higher Self. The Sema {Yoga} of Action enhances and harnesses the movement and behavior aspect in a human personality and directs it towards the Higher Self. The Sema {Yoga} of Meditation enhances and harnesses the willing aspect in a human personality and directs it towards the Higher Self. The willing aspect of human personality may be defined as that which involves resolution, determination, resolve, choice and volition.

The process of spiritual life means turning away from the negative aspects of consciousness and turning towards the positive or lucid aspects, which lead to enlightenment. The waking state is the most concrete state and as such, it acts to anchor the soul to a physical form (human body) over an extended period of time, and through it the soul encounters various experiences, which will provide pleasure and pain. It is not possible to practice the spiritual disciplines of Sema {Yoga} and mystical religion in the dream state or the sleep state. Thus, the waking - physical state is the field in which the *Emotion, Reason, Action* and *Will* of a human being can be played out in an extended format of time and space, unlike the dream plane in which an entire world can come into existence and vanish in a flash. So the task of spiritual disciplines is to engage in practices (virtues) which will promote a movement towards lucidity (wisdom-enlightenment) and move away from the activities, thoughts and feelings which promote agitation, distraction, discontent and ultimately lead to the state of *Dullness* and ignorance of the intellect. This process entails controlling anger, hatred, greed, etc., and promoting effacement of the ego through righteous actions, simplicity, truthfulness, patience and other virtues.

Once a spiritual aspirant has worked on promoting *Lucidity* in the waking state by controlling the Agitating factors which lead to the state of *Agitation* such as distraction, desire, longing, anger, hatred, greed, lust, etc., it is possible, with a mind that is calm, lucid and strong willed, to practice formal meditation on the innermost Self. When this level of spiritual practice is reached such a person is considered to be advanced on the spiritual path. Their powers of concentration, fortitude and inner peace they have gained through intellectual knowledge has allowed them to develop real faith through which they can understand the goal of spirituality and exert the necessary self-effort needed to realize the objective. Already they are far elevated from the masses of people who live to satisfy their desires for the limited enjoyments which the world seems to bring. Their constantly agitated state of mind precludes reflectiveness and inner peace, without which it is not possible to discover the inner meaning of spirituality. Their understanding is shallow, intellectual, theoretical and their will power is weak, so they do not desire for spiritual emancipation. As a result they are caught up in the activities, desires and longings of modern society.

## SUCCESS IN CONCENTRATION

It is important to understand that concentration of mind is the most difficult aspect of meditation practice because most people have led distracted lives and the mind is used to being distracted. You must practice your concentration efforts even if it seems as though you are not achieving any progress. Eventually your mind will calm down and you will achieve success. This may take time (weeks or months).

## *Stages in the Practice of GLM Meditation*

The Glorious Light Meditation practice is given in four stages or disciplines.

**1-Myth,** In this practice myth is important because it holds the essential keys to the wisdom for understanding the mind and the spiritual journey. The forms of the myth act as anchors for the mind to aid in the concentration efforts but must be eventually transcended. This is the outer practice; Then come the internalized (Formal) practices. This is why the teaching specifically instructs that the myth is to be recited before the practice. It prepares the mind to accept the *Ra Akhu* {Glorious Light} through the practice of the formal meditation by disciplining the mind through *Concentration, and Meditation,* which allow the mind to reach and experience *Transcendental Consciousness* repeatedly.

**2-Concentration,**

**3-Meditation** (extended, effortless concentration-mind flowing towards the Divine automatically,

**4-Transcendental Consciousness** (unity with the transcendent).

## Steps to Practice the Glorious Light Meditation

To Begin: Be seated or lie down in a relaxed pose. See the diagram provided for the location of the energy centers. Visualize yourself gaining cosmic energy. See it accumulating in the body. Place your concentration on the first energy center at the base of the spine as you inhale. See the energy tapping that spot, then see it rising through the other energy centers going up to the sixth center where the pineal gland is situated (The Uraeus). Exhale and see the energy go back down to the first center. Inhale and repeat the exercise. Feel the increasing levels of PEACE *(htp)* develop.

The highest form of meditation is maintaining a perennial awareness of the supreme truth which transcends all other realities. This truth is that God is the underlying reality behind all things and most importantly, that the innermost reality of your own heart is none other than the Absolute Supreme Self which transcends time, space, thought and the ego. The meditation presented below outlines a format for a formal sit-down meditation in which the meditator is directed to see himself or herself as the Supreme Being (Ra). This is a most powerful visualization for meditation practice.

As stated earlier, the oldest known formal meditation instruction comes from the Ancient Egyptian story of "The Destruction of Evil Men and Women". The following lines of scripture are from the original text translations. The meditation is to be practiced after listening to and having gained an understanding of the teachings presented in the myth and then following the instructions contained in the concluding portion of the story of the scripture.

## Study of the Hieroglyphic Text of the

## Glorious Light Meditation

What follows is a translation and detailed study of selected sections of the hieroglyphic text of the Glorious Light Meditation instructions given by the ancient Egyptian Sages. Mythologically, it was created by Djehuty for Hetheru. As Hetheru is symbolic of anyone who reads the story it follows that anyone practicing the meditation assumes the role of Hetheru, her downfall and eventual enlightenment. Thus, every follower of this teaching becomes Hetheru, being taught by Djehuty, on their way to discovering their true identity as Ra. The Study is presented as an interlinear transliteration with a word for word translation for easy understanding.

# The Glorious Light Meditation

*Yar-un-n ab n Djehuty r shed st her Ra*
Whoever  in heart of Djehuty reads words these for Ra

*Ab        cher-f mt        sefech heru chmt iri hmu remtge*
Cleansing presence his purifications 7, days 3  to be done by clergy and men
and women

*mitt        iry   ir shedds   iri-f   iru        pennty   irit*
alike.        Wherefore reading    done   Divine(figure) form these     do
ritual (rite)

*meht-n iuf iri-f ahau  maq  b-phr      nty    hau            iu*
read   body  do   make stand, protection legs surrounded by, expansion and
within the Sundisk (circle of Ra)

*irii-f  er-f  at –f neb-r-f  n sny  shm  mtu-f. Iu    djedmedu   in*
eyes  attention body parts all of same person, not pass by, going away body.
Now words to be spoken by

*remteg        Iuf     mi  Ra    heru   mestu-f          n-shry   chet*
people*        "Body  is like Ra's day    birth his          not diminishing objects

*n     sat      shry  reryt            shes  ma heh*
not   wisdom or diminishing house of person bound, righteousness millions"**
*f– refers to male and female. **years

The preceding may be thus rendered as follows:

*Whosoever shall recite the words, here written, with consciousness awareness of Djehuty {mind with clear and keen intellect} shall perform the rituals of sevenfold purification over three days {the seven psychospiritual consciousness centers}[5] which are to be performed in the Divine presence, when this book is being read {studied, recited, remembered}.(1) And they shall make their position in a circle which is beyond them, and their two eyes shall be focused upon themselves, all their members shall be composed,* [relaxed, motionless] *and their steps shall not carry them away* [from the place of meditation].(2) *Whoever among men shall recite* [these] *words shall visualize themselves as Ra on the day of his birth; and their awareness shall not become contracted, and his house shall never fall into decay, but shall endure in truth and righteousness for eternity.(3)*

Instructions form the Hieroglyphic Text

*(1)-Posture and Focus of Attention*

Posture is one of the main components of the meditation practice. This text prescribes a sitting position within a circle. Then it instructs that there should be a focusing of the mind between the eye brows. This area is also known as the sixth energy-consciousness center where the Uraeus serpent, the Eye of Ra and the Udjat, the Eye of Heru, are located. All the members of the body, the arms, legs, etc. should be motionless.

**Posture:** Be seated in a comfortable posture. You may create a circle figure in which to sit or simply visualize that you are seated within a circle. See yourself at the center of the circle which comprises the Sundisk of Ra, ⊙, and see yourself as the source of all that is. The place you use for meditation should be clean and free from drafts, dimly lit (preferably use a candle to

---

[5] This book contains a basic introduction and practice of the discipline of *the seven psychospiritual consciousness centers (Serpent Power). For the more advanced understanding see the books The Serpent Power* and *The Kemetic Tree of Life* by Muata Ashby and consult with your meditation teacher.

symbolize the inner light. Incense may be used also. Use a mat, sitting comfortably with back straight. This special area should be used only for meditation and you should practice at the same time daily.

## MEDITATION POSTURES

At left:
The Lotus posture

At left:
The seated position with arms resting on the thighs.

Below:
the Corpse pose.

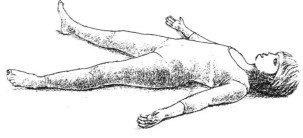

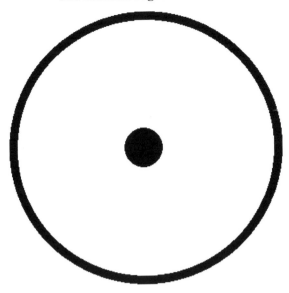

Instruction: Visualize the symbol of Ra and Hetheru in your mind's eye. Make stand within the Sundisk ( circle of Ra) for protection, your legs being surrounded by it.

### Introduction to The Seven-fold Cleansing, the Serpent Power and the Teaching of the Life Force:

The concept of the Serpent Power, a Life Force contained in the subtle body of a human being that operates through the nervous system of the subtle spine and which has seven primary foci of energy consciousness comes down through Ancient Kamitan history from the Great Sphinx to the teaching of the Asarian Resurrection and is iconographically expressed central shaft of the balance scales of Maat, in the pillar of Asar and in the Caduceus of Djehuti (contained in his staff {a central shaft with two serpents}, a caduceus formed by the divinities Asar (his backbone) and the two serpent goddesses Aset and Nebthet. The movement of the Serpent Power/Life Force is described in the special text.[6] The *Sefekh Ba Ra* (energy centers) or "seven souls of Ra", wherein the Life Force energy and consciousness are transformed from subtle to gross energy for use by the body are seven in number and are depicted as follows.

**Figure 19: Below- Left-The Ancient Egyptian Papyrus Greenfield (British Museum).**

**Figure 20: Above right-Papyrus Qenna (Leyden Museum), displaying the rings signifying the serpentine path of the Life Force from the Spirit above to the heart below, and the levels of spiritual consciousness (the Chakras or Psycho-spiritual consciousness centers)**

---

[6] translated in the book *The Serpent* by Muata Ashby)

## The Energy Centers of the Subtle Body

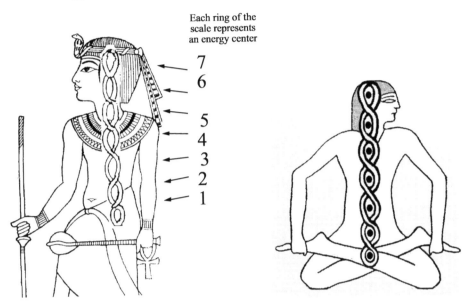

Above- artistic representation of an Ancient Egyptian displaying the "chains" (intertwining serpents) of the *Arat Shekhem* (Serpent Power) and the *Sefech Ba Ra* (seven spheres or Life Force energy centers) based on the Greenfield Papyrus.

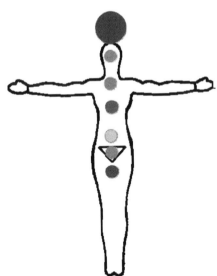

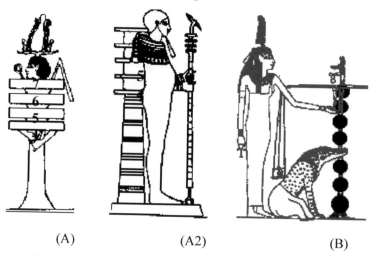

(A)                    (A2)                    (B)

**Center (A 1-2), Ptah-Asar-Ancient Egyptian rendition of the Life Force energy centers in the subtle spine of the individual. The god Asar displays the four upper centers as centers of higher consciousness.**

*The figure at right (B) shows the scale of Maat displaying the seven spheres or energy centers called the "seven souls of Ra" and "the seven arms of the balance (Maat)."*

Figure (B), above, includes the Ammit demon, (composite beast combining one third hippopotamus, one third lion and one third crocodile), symbolic devourer of unrighteous souls, biting between the $3^{rd}$ & $4^{th}$ sphere (energy center-chakra). This means that those who have not attained a consciousness level higher than the $3^{rd}$ center will continue to suffer and reincarnate. The spheres represent levels of spiritual consciousness from the most ignorant (1) to the most enlightened (7). The lower three spheres are related to worldly consciousness and the upper four are related to spiritual consciousness and enlightenment, therefore, the lower must be sublimated into the higher levels. This is the project of spiritual evolution. Those who have attained higher ($3^{rd}$ through the $7^{th}$) will move on and attain enlightenment. This Kamitan system of energy spheres and the Caduceus with its central shaft symbolizing the subtle spine, and the two intertwining serpents, symbolizing the dual energies into which the central shaft differentiates, concurs in every detail with the later developments in East Indian Mysticism encompassed by the discipline known as Kundalini Yoga with its system of Chakras and the three main energy channels, Sushumna (central) and Ida and Pingala (intertwining conduits). For more details on the Serpent Power see the books *The Serpent Power* and *The Kemetic Tree of Life* by Muata Ashby

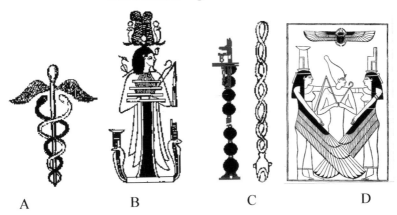

| A | B | C | D |

Above A- the Hermetic[7] Caduceus with the central Shaft (Asar), and the intertwining serpents (Uadjit and Nekhebit, also known as Aset and Nebethet);

Above B-Ancient caduceus motif: Asar with the serpent goddesses.

Above C- The Kamitan Energy Consciousness Centers (depicted as Spheres-Chakras or serpentine chains)

Above D- The God Asar is embraced by goddesses Nebethet (left) and Aset (right) in the caduceus posture.

---

[7] Late Ancient Egyptian motif.

## The Glorious Light translation Continued: The Special Words to be Uttered:

*Rdjer-f Medu      si    iri-f   makt*
Whoever   speaks  self  makes  protection

*Fm    hekau       nuk    Hekau       pui     ab*
Through words of power: I am   Hekau        this God  pure

*Im    rai   khati  Ra   neteru  depry wat     n-rai      Nuk*
Within  2 mouths  body  Ra  gods and  who is their  of my mouth   I
                            goddesses    way                      am

*Ra    Akhu       medu-k ywkmmash ru       manu   uben-her*
Ra's  glorious spirit  speak    move on    in the evening  and  day as a
                       these words                         shining {light}
                                                           personality

*Her  er  kft      n    Ra    Nuk    Ba    f    Hekau*
[Persons as to enemies] of Ra    I am      Soul  his   Hekau I am!
[Dealing with thee will fall]

The preceding may be thus rendered as follows:

*The words of power of the scripture and the chant are a special protection {against unrighteousness and negativity}. Through the words of power <u>"Nuk Hekau"</u> {I am the Divinity of the word} the divinity purifies in the two mouths of Ra {phenomenal/transcendental} gods and goddesses such that <u>"Nuk Ra Akhu"</u> {I am Ra's Glorious Spirit [Light]}. As Ra I move in the evening and the day as a shining Spirit {living (in light) and not in death (darkness). Enemies of the light {unrighteousness, darkness, ignorance, vices, etc.} fall because <u>Nuk Ba Ra Hekau</u> {I am the soul of Ra, the Divine Word, that transforms (into the Shining Spirit [the Glorious Light].*

### (2)- Words of power

"Devote yourself to adore God's name."
—Ancient Egyptian Proverb

The papyrus instructs that after having read and recited the story one should assume a specific posture and adopt a specific visualization. The story in the papyrus (Destruction of Humankind) is as follows.

Ra (Supreme Being) created the world and human beings. After many years they became arrogant and spoke evilly about him. They forgot about his greatness and about their own origins. Ra decided to punish them for their egoism and sinful behavior and so he sent out his eye of destruction in the form of Hetheru to kill all sinners. He then recalled his eye before it could kill all human beings and then He retreated to heaven where he traverses in the form of the sun and installed his vicar to watch over the world during the night in the form of the moon.*

Thus, Ra is the creator of this entire universe and it is sustained by him at all times. This Supreme Self, Ra, is the same essence which abides in the heart of every human being. This is confirmed by the *Ancient Egyptian Book of Coming Forth By Day* in Chapter 17. Therefore, having this knowledge, one should understand that one's Higher Self is in reality not the limited and transient human personality but the Supreme Self. Therefore, one who understands this teaching should see himself or herself as that very same Self. The words of power which affirm this understanding are: ***Nuk Ra*** "I am Ra" (the Supreme Divinity).

## Hekau - Words of Power - Chanting
### Reciting words of power is like making a well.

**Hekau**

**Number per minute**

**Number per hour**

| Kemetic Chants and the frequency of practice in formal meditation chanting. | Low | Med | High | Low | Med | High |
|---|---|---|---|---|---|---|
| Om | 140 | 250 | 400 | 8400 | 15000 | 24000 |
| Om Asar Aset Heru | 80 | 120 | 140 | 4800 | 7200 | 9000 |
| amma su en pa neter sauu - k su emment en pa neter au duanu ma qedi pa haru | 6 | 8 | 10 | 360 | 480 | 600 |
| Nuk Hekau*Nuk Ra AkhuNuk Ba RaNuk Hekau | 4 | 8 | 16 | 240 | 480 | 600 |

*Words of Power for Glorious Light Meditation system

131

## Chanting the Divine Name

The word *"mantra"* in Indian Yoga signifies any sound which steadies the mind. Its roots are: "man" which means "mind" and "tra" which means "steady". In Ancient Egyptian terminology, "hekau" or word formulas are recited with meaning and feeling to achieve the desired end.

Hekau-mantra recitation, (called *Japa* in India), is especially useful in changing the mental state. The sounds coupled with ideas or meditations can have the effect of calming the mind by directing its energy toward sublime thoughts rather than toward degrading, pain filled ones. This allows the vibrations of the mind to be changed. There are three types of recitations that can be used with the words of power: 1- Mental, 2- Recitation employing a soft humming sound and 3- loud or audible reciting. The main purpose of reciting the words of power is somewhat different than prayer. Prayer involves you as a subject, "talking" to God, while words of power - hekau - mantras, are used to carry your consciousness to divine levels by changing the vibrations in your mind and allowing it to transcend the awareness of the senses, body and ordinary thought processes.

The recitation of words of power has been explored to such a degree that it constitutes an important form of yoga practice. Two of the most comprehensive books written on this subject by Sri Swami Sivananda were *Japa Yoga* and *Sadhana*. Swami Sivananda told his pupils to repeat their mantras as many as 50,000 per day. If this level of practice is maintained, it is possible to achieve specific changes in a short time. Otherwise, changes in your level of mental awareness, self-control, mental peace and spiritual realization occur according to your level of practice. You should not rush nor suppress your spiritual development, rather allow it to gradually grow into a fire which engulfs the mind as your spiritual aspiration grows in a natural way.

Hekau-mantras can be directed toward worldly attainments or toward spiritual attainment in the form of enlightenment. Reciting words of power is like making a well. If a well is made deep enough, it yields water. If the words of power are used long enough and with consistency, they yield spiritual vibrations which reach deep into the unconscious mind to cut through the distracting thoughts and then reveal the deeper you. If they are not used with consistency, they are like shallow puddles which get filled easily by rain, not having had a chance to go deeply enough to reveal what lies within. Don't forget that your movement in Sema {Yoga} should be balanced and integrated. Therefore, continue your practice of the other major disciplines we have described along with your practice of reciting the hekau-mantras. Mental recitation is considered to be the most powerful. However, in the beginning you may need to start with recitation aloud until you are able to control the mind's wandering. If it wanders, simply return to the words of power (hekau-mantras). Eventually the words of power will develop their own staying power. You will even hear them when you are not consciously reciting. They will begin to replace the negative thought patterns of the mind and lead the mind toward serenity and from here to spiritual realization. When this occurs you should allow yourself to feel the sweetness of reciting the divine names.

As discussed earlier, HEKAU may be used to achieve control over the mind and to develop the latent forces that are within you. Hekau or mantras are mystic formulas which an aspirant uses in a process of self-alchemy. The chosen words of power may be in the form of a letter, word or a combination of words which hold a specific mystical meaning to lead the mind to deeper levels of concentration and to deeper levels of understanding of the teaching behind the words. You may choose one for yourself or you may use one that you were initiated into by a spiritual preceptor. Also, you may have a special hekau for meditation and you may still use other hekau, prayers, hymns or songs of praise according to your devotional feeling. Once you choose a hekau, the practice involves its repetition with meaning and feeling to the point of becoming one with it. You will experience that the words of power drop from your mind and there are no thoughts but just awareness. This is the soul level where you begin to transcend thoughts and body identification. You may begin practicing it out loud (verbally) and later practice in silence (mentally). At some point your level of concentration will deepen. You may use a rosary or "mala" (beads on a string) to keep track of your recitation. At that point your mind will disengage from all external exercises and take flight into the unknown, uncharted waters of the subconscious, the unconscious, and beyond. Simply remain as a detached witness and allow yourself to grow in peace. Listed below is the hekau taken from Ancient Egyptian "Destruction of Unrighteous Men and Women and The Story of Hetheru and Djehuty". It may be used in English or in ancient Kemetic according to your choice.

If you feel a certain affinity toward a particular energy expressed through a particular divinity, use that inclination to your advantage by aligning yourself with that energy and then directing it toward the divine within your heart. Never forget that while you are working with a particular divinity (in this case Ra) in the beginning stages, your objective is to delve into the deeper mystical implications of the symbolic form and characteristics of the divinity (The transcendental Self, which is represented by the image of Ra). These always refer to the transcendental Self which is beyond all divinities. According to your level of advancement you may construct your own Hekau according to your own feeling and understanding. As a rule, in meditations such as those being discussed now, the shorter the size of the hekau the more effective it will be since you will be able repeat it more often in a shorter period of time. However, the shorter the hekau, the more concentration it requires so as not to get lost in thoughts. You may wish to begin with a longer hekau and shorten it as your concentration builds. Words of power have no power in and of themselves. It is the user who imbues them power through understanding and feeling and usage.

The heart of the Glorious Light Meditation is identification with the Glorious Light of the Self. When practicing the devout ritual identification form of meditation, the recitation of hymns, the wearing of costumes and elaborate amulets and other artifacts may be used. Ritual identification with the divine may be practiced by studying and repeatedly reading the various hymns to the divine such as those which have been provided in this volume, while gradually absorbing and becoming one with the teachings as they relate to you. When a creation hymn is being studied, you should reflect upon it as your true Self being the Creator, as your true Self being the hero (heroine), and that you (your true essence) are the one being spoken about in all the teachings. It is all about you. "You" are the Creator. "You" are the sustainer of the universe. "You" are the only one who can achieve transcendence through enlightenment according to your own will. When you feel, think and act this way, you are using the highest form of worship and meditation toward the divine by constantly bringing the mind back to the idea that all is the Self and that you essentially are that Self. This form of practice is higher than any ritual or any other kind of offering. Here you are concentrating on the idea that your limited personality is only an expression of the divine. You are laying down your ego on the offering mat.

Generally, when the words of power are used over a sustained period of time, the benefits or psychic powers arise. The most important psychic powers you can attain to facilitate your spiritual program are peace, serenity of mind, and concentration of the mental vibrations. Concentration opens the door to transcendental awareness and spiritual realization. Various estimates are given as to when you may expect to feel results; these vary from 500,000 repetitions to 1,200,000 or more. The number should not be your focus. Sustained practice, understanding the teachings about the Self and practicing of the virtues and self-control in an integral, balanced fashion are the most important factors determining your eventual success.

While *Om* is most commonly known as a *Sanskrit* mantra (word of power from India), it also appears in the Ancient Egyptian texts and is closely related to the Kemetic *Amun* in sound and Amen of Christianity. More importantly, it has the same meaning as Amun and is therefore completely compatible with the energy pattern of the entire group. According to the Egyptian Leyden papyrus, the name of the "Hidden God", referring to Amun, may be pronounced as *Om,* or *Am.* Om is a powerful sound; it represents the primordial sound of creation. Thus it appears in Ancient Egypt as Om, in modern day India as Om, and in Christianity as Amen, being derived from Amun. Om may also be used for engendering mental calm prior to beginning recitation of a longer set of words of power or it may be used alone as described above. One Indian Tantric scripture (*Tattva*

*Prakash*) states that Om or AUM can be used to achieve the mental state free of physical identification and can bring union with *Brahman* (the Absolute transcendental Supreme Being - God) if it is repeated 300,000 times. In this sense, mantras such as Om, Soham, Sivoham, Aham Brahmasmi are called *Moksha Mantras* or mantras which lead to union with the Absolute Self. Their shortness promotes greater concentration and force toward the primordial level of consciousness. Begin your spiritual practice with an invocation to Ra:

*Iuf    mi Ra   heru  mestu-f      n-shry   chet*
"My body  is like Ra's on the  day of his birth  not diminishing objects
*n     sat       shry   reryt       shes  ma heh*
not  wisdom  diminishing or house of person bound, righteousness endures

The Hekau prescribed by the ancient Egyptian Sages for use with the Glorious Light Meditation is:

>    *Nuk Hekau* (I am the word* itself)
>    *Nuk Ra Akhu* (I am Ra's Glorious Shinning** Spirit)
>    *Nuk Ba Ra* (I am the soul of Ra)
>    *Nuk Hekau* (I am the God who creates*** through sound)

*The "Word" in mystical philosophy is the power of vibration. All things are seen as being engendered through vibration. The sages of ancient times knew this and now in modern physics this understanding has been confirmed. Thus, through utterance of sound God created the universe and in the same manner by utterance of certain sounds human beings can create spiritual enlightenment or human degradation. Through the special words given above the spiritual aspirant will create the awareness of their oneness with the Glorious Divine Self (Ra) and thereby attain spiritual enlightenment.

**Ra means Divine Light. Akhu literally refers to the aspect of the personality that is the inner light, as the light that illumines the mind when the eyes are closes and you are in a dark room. Akhu is the glorified light, the spirit which illumines your thoughts. It is your higher Self, the reason why you can think, and even exist.

***In ancient Kemetic mystical philosophy "Hekau" is seen as the words of power themselves, as a vibratory, creative force as described above, but also as a divinity or Neteru, a god or cosmic force. Therefore, the utterance of those special words of power not only means the invocation of their power but also that one embodies their divine essence as well. Further, it should be kept in mind that the god Hekau is an aspect of Ra, his soul.

135

The Words of Power of the Glorious Light Meditation should be uttered together when used in formal practice. However, at other times you may choose a segment of the chant for easy practice. See the chanting frequency chart for additional instructions. During your practice of the chant you will come to a place where the chant stops naturally and your mind will be empty. This is different from losing the chant due to the mind straying into worldly thoughts. You will feel light, transcendental and at peace and eventually you will even transcend these feelings altogether. Do not attempt to think or bring the chant back. Simply experience the purity of consciousness, the Glorious light.

---

*(3)- Visualization*

**Spiritual Realization**
(Merging with the Divine - experiencing the Self)

**Devotional Meditation**
(I am one with God.)

**Worship**
(Seeing God in everything; practicing spiritual disciplines - prayer, meditation, selfless service, etc.)

↑

**Learning**
(Learning about the Divine through myths and mystical philosophy.)

---

Visualization is the next important element in this meditation instruction. The form of visualization to be practiced here is called: *Ritual Identification with the Divine Self.* Ritual Identification falls under the category of Sema {Yoga} of Devotion. As explained throughout this text, the ordinary form of identification people have, that is, their idea of who they are, is an egoistic notion based on ignorance of the deeper Self within. This form of visualization should be practiced at all times as a perpetual mindfulness exercise, as well as when practicing a formal meditation session.

The Glorious Light Meditation incorporates the Yoga of Devotional Love and the Yoga of Wisdom as well as the Yoga of Meditation. It consists of understanding and directing the feelings and emotions towards the Divine Self who abides in all Creation. When you love something, you put that object first, even before your own desires. Through this process of sublimating your own desires and directing the mind towards the Divine, the ego begins to diminish, and this process allows the mind to soar high among the sublime feelings and thoughts. Devotion leads to wisdom and like two wings of a bird, the spiritual aspirant is led from faith to knowledge and then to experience the Divine. Therefore, the Myth of the Destruction of Unrighteous Men and Women and the Story of Hetheru and Djehuty should be recited or read prior to the formal practice of the Glorious Light Meditation.

It is important to understand that devotional Sema {Yoga} involves more than simply mindlessly or fanatically praising God and praying or singing devotional songs with emotional force. An integrated process of Devotional Yoga involves an understanding of the metaphysical teachings of wisdom and a blending of all of the other Yogic systems. This integrated process which involves wisdom or intuitional understanding of the metaphysical realities behind Creation serves to close any gaps in the mind of the aspirant as to the existence of the Divine. In this meditation the aspirant is directed to identify himself/herself with the Supreme Being in the form of birth. This form is known as *Khepri*, and symbolizes the emerging spiritual birth of the Divine within the human heart.

**To aid your visualization:** you may compose an altar with special spiritual icons that will help you to focus your mind: a candle, sundisk symbol, pictures or statues of Ra, Hetheru and or Djehuty or anything else which helps you to remember the teachings and causes your mind to flow towards calm and peace. Therefore, after performing the necessary ablutions of mind and body and outer preparations of your meditation area, meditate thus:

**Visualization:** See yourself as the transformative power which gives life to all things. See yourself as the sustainer of creation. See yourself as the being into which the creation dissolves in order to give way to a new cycle of creation. You are not just the body, but you encompass the entire universe. This is your true possession. Even though the world may come into existence, decay and die, you do not decay, or die, and neither are you born. You are the immortal, transcendental Self. You are the beginning, middle and end. You have existed from immeasurable time and will exist for eternity. You are one with the Absolute!

## ADVANCING THE PRACTICE – ADDING THE SEVENFOLD CLEANSING

**Putting it All Together:** Having remembered the myth of Hetheru and Djehuty sit quietly within your circle and begin the chant of the GLM as you exhale: *Nuk Hekau, Nuk Ra Akhu, Nuk Ba Ra, Nuk Hekau...*

Now as you inhale utter the chant internally with the inhalation...

Now again chant audibly as you exhale...

As you coordinate the chant and breath and become more comfortable and firm in the posture add the following visualization to your practice. This is the sevenfold cleansing. Visualize a golden light at the base of your spine and as you begin the chant with the first "Nuk" see that light at the first "Ba Ra" (Sphere)...

See the light rising up through each Ba Ra until you reach the sphere at the crown of your head as you at the same time end the whole chant … *Nuk Hekau, Nuk Ra Akhu, Nuk Ba Ra, Nuk Hekau…*

Now, as you begin the chant again visualize that light moving downward to the base of the spine as you are chanting… *Nuk Hekau, Nuk Ra Akhu, Nuk Ba Ra, Nuk Hekau…*

Along with this practice reflect that the negative thoughts, feelings and deeds represented by each energy center is being cleansed. The objective is to allo the positive to express by clearing away the negative related to each principle. 1-base of the spine: Principles *Earth, food, materialism.* 2-perineum: Principles *sex, worldly desires.* 3-solar plexus: Principle *egoism.* 4-heart, Principle *empathy.* 5-throat: Principles *self-will, speech.* 6-forehead: Principle *duality.* 7-crown of the head: Principle *transcendence.* This practice enhances concentration on the self and cleanses the subtle psycho-spiritual energy centers, preparing the way for higher consciousness.

## SILENCE TIME

You should strive to practice the GLM for a minimum of 20 minutes daily. As you advance, after some time of practicing the visualization, chant and breath you may be elevated into the astral plane and you will lose awareness of the physical body and only awareness of mind remains. You may survey what you find in this realm but it is not the ultimate goal so you should not linger there even though it is after a while a comfortable and wonderous place to be. As you continue this meditative discipline will be elevated to a place of silence, the realm called: *anrutef.* In this special level of consciousness one can discover the nature of self beyond mind ands senses most intensely, for *anrutef* means "the place where nothing grows. There are no distracting thoughts or desires there, just radiant transcendental experience with, in, one with, the *glorious light.* How does this work?

When one attains establishment ⌐⌐, *men,* in higher knowledge ⊖𝄇 *rech,* then one is said to have opened the Divine Eye 👁 *Arit,* and raised the serpent power ⟨ *arat,* which has coursed up through and perched atop the ⫞ *Djed* pillar which is the subtle spine. This entire process leads to attaining ⟡ *akhu,* illumination and self-knowledge: ⊙𝄇⟡ ⟡ *rech-i em ib-i,* "Know I in heart mine," or "I know what is in my heart" i.e. "I know myself." And self-knowledge leads to ⟰⟡⌂👁 *Nehast* or resurrection, i.e. Spiritual Enlightenment.

138

*anrutef -growthless, barren.*

So, when the higher level of consciousness is reached it is not necessary to practice the visualization and chant or the breath. That would be stepping down from the heights. So the emphasis here is now on silence and contemplation. This is being immersed in the Ba of Ra, which eventually, as it did for Lady Aset, bestows spiritual enlightenment, discovery of the true nature of Self. For more on the advancing practice consult with your meditation instructor.

# SUMMARY OF THE TEACHING OF THE GLORIOUS LIGHT MEDITATION

Formal meditation in Sema {Yoga} consists of some basic elements: Posture, Sound (chant-words of power), Visualization, Rhythmic Breathing (calm, steady breath). The instructions, translated from the original hieroglyphic text contain the basic elements for formal meditation.

---

**Basic Instructions for the Glorious Light Meditation System- Given in the Tomb of Seti I.**
**(c. 1350 B.C.E.)**

---

Basic instructions given in the text:

1. **To Be Practiced by Clergy and Lay Alike**

2. **Listen to the Mystical Teaching** in the Myth of Hetheru and Djehuty

3. **Be purified physically by proper hygiene**-with Nile Flood Water (cleanest); wear proper clothing.

4. **Be purified by Maat** (righteousness, truth, Non-violence, non-stealing, non-killing, etc.)

5. **Sevenfold Cleansing for three days**- Serpent Power – transcend the three forms of mental expression

6. **Posture and Focus of Attention** - Make the body still, concentrating on yourself

7. **Words of power-chant**
   *Nuk Hekau* (I am the word itself –that purifies)
   *Nuk Ra Akhu* (I am Ra's Glorious Shinning Spirit – Divine Light)
   *Nuk Ba Ra* (I am the soul of Ra)
   *Nuk Hekau* (I am the God who creates through sound)

8. **Visualization**- see yourself in the center of the Sundisk (circle of Ra), see yourself as Ra (Mystic Union)

---

140

# Additional Hieroglyphic Terms related to the GLM

### 3) THE AKH:

The hieroglyph of the word Khu is the "crested ibis." The ibis is representative symbol of Djehuty the god of reason and knowledge. As such it relates to the pure spiritual essence of a human being that is purified by lucidity of mind. The Akh is the spirit, which is immortal; it is associated with the Ba and is an Ethereal Being. The Akh is also referred to as the "being of light" or "luminous being." The Akh illumines the personality and without this light the personality and the mind cannot function. It is the light of consciousness itself.

Wake up Awake- *Nehas*

Enlightenment- *Nehast*

Resurrection, spiritual

To Know-understand- *Såa.*

**Agitated, disturbed-** *Neshsh*

Sluggard, lazy, innert, dull man- *Neni.*

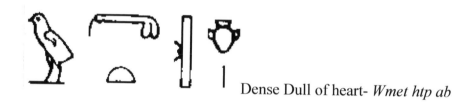

Dense Dull of heart- *Wmet htp ab*

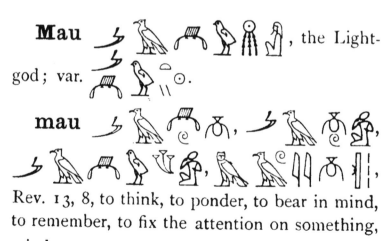

**Mau** , the Light-god; var. .

**mau** , , , Rev. 13, 8, to think, to ponder, to bear in mind, to remember, to fix the attention on something, mind, memory

**Maut** , , light, radiance, brilliance, splendour

# Video and Audio Seminar Workshop Series Presentation of The Glorious Light Meditation System

Glorious Light Meditation System of Ancient Egypt

**VIDEO LECTURE $20.00 Introduction to the Glorious Light Meditation System of Ancient Egypt**

**FREE VIDEO: Available Online at:** www.GloriousLightMeditation.org

**AUDIO LECTURE SERIES: Meditation Lectures Series and Technique Directly Based on Ancient Egyptian Scriptures:**

Available via Digital Download at: www.GloriousLightMeditation.org

6001A Introduction to the Glorious Light Meditation Part 1
6001B Introduction to the Glorious Light Meditation Part 2
6002A Insights into the practice of Meditation Part 1
6002B Insights into the practice of Meditation Part 2
6003    Insights into the myth of Hetheru and Djehuty
6004    Insights into the myth of Hetheru and Djehuty
6005A The Steps of the Glorious Light Meditation Technique Part 1
6005B The Steps of the Glorious Light Meditation Technique Part 2
6005C The Steps of the Glorious Light Meditation Technique Part 3
6006A Waking Up to the Higher Self Through Detachment Part 1
6006B Waking Up to the Higher Self Through Detachment Part 2
6006C Waking Up to the Higher Self Through Detachment Part 3
6007A Glorious Light Meditation Session
6007B Glorious Light Meditation Session Q and A

6100   Glorious Light Meditation Session 1/30/00

## Music and Recorded Chant for the GLM practice:

The Glorious Light Meditation   $14.99

**Available Through**
**Cruzian Mystic Books**
**305-378-6253**
www.GloriousLightMeditation.org
**www.Egyptianyoga.com**

# The Glorious Light Meditation Mat

Ra Akhu: Glorious Light Blanket/Mat (throw) 4' X 6' 100% Cotton with image on both sides. Specially designed by Sebai MAA for use with the Glorious Light Meditation Based on the book The Glorious Light Meditation of Ancient Egypt

Here is a design made now with the essential teaching of the Ra-Akhu Uaa: Glorious-Light-Meditation discipline including the hekau of GLM Nuk Hekau, Nuk Ra Akhu, Nuk Ba Ra, Nuk Hekau and the geometric diagrams of the path as enjoined in the scripture as well as the names of the main divinities and the central symbol of Ra for making the "stand" (posture for meditation) within- includes the special final declaration of the scripture for all who practice this teaching- similar in construction to the Maat and Anpu blankets you have already seen - 48 x 70 inches. Gold and Black. It is designed for meditation practice. The practitioners is to sit in the circle with the mat facing to the west.

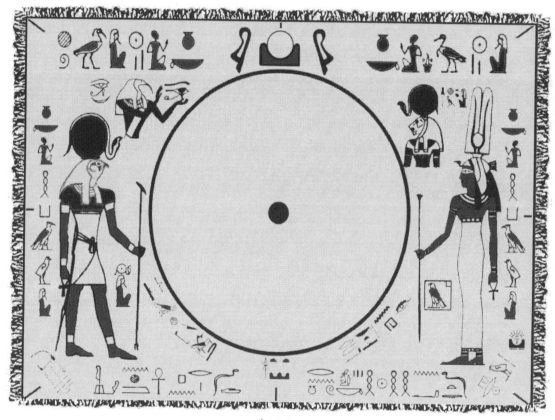

$45.00
www.GloriousLightMeditation.org
www.Egyptianyoga.com
**(305) 378-6253, Fax. (305) 378-6253**

# INDEX

secrets of the universe, 27

See also Ra-Hrakti, 1, 10, 11, 12, 26, 29, 33, 34, 35, 36, 37, 38, 45, 46, 47, 48, 49, 50, 51, 54, 55, 56, 59, 60, 64, 65, 67, 68, 69, 70, 71, 72, 73, 80, 81, 82, 84, 85, 96, 97, 98, 99, 102, 104, 109, 111, 118, 119, 121, 123, 124, 125, 129, 130, 131, 133, 135, 137, 138, 139, 140, 144, 163, 173, 175

**See Nat**, 175

Sekhem, 46, 154

Sekhemit, 46, 50

Self (see Ba, soul, Spirit, Universal, Ba, Neter, Heru)., 2, 10, 11, 20, 21, 29, 31, 36, 37, 39, 41, 45, 66, 67, 68, 69, 71, 72, 73, 75, 76, 78, 79, 80, 81, 84, 85, 89, 90, 91, 92, 93, 94, 96, 97, 98, 99, 100, 104, 107, 109, 111, 114, 115, 116, 117, 119, 130, 133, 134, 135, 136, 137, 139, 143, 158, 161, 162, 163

Self (seeBasoulSpiritUniversal BaNeterHorus)., 29

Self-created lifestyle, lifestyle, 93

Self-realization, 11

self-sufficiency, 101

Sema, 2, 3, 11, 25, 27, 41, 66, 69, 73, 74, 86, 87, 95, 103, 107, 110, 116, 132, 136, 137, 140, 160, 176

Sema Tawi, 25, 27, 41

Senses, 21

Serpent, 10, 46, 87, 97, 121, 124, 125, 126, 140

Serpent Power, 10, 46, 87, 97, 121, 124, 125, 126, 140

Serpent Power (see also Kundalini and Buto), 10, 46, 87, 97, 121, 124, 125, 126, 140

Serpent Power see also Kundalini Yoga, 10, 46, 87, 97, 121, 124, 125, 126, 140

Set, 27, 39, 41, 48, 75, 78, 82, 107

Seti I, 11, 12, 13, 14, 16, 17, 26, 113, 140, 163, 175

Setian, 107

Seven, 124

seven souls of Ra, see also Sefek ba Ra, 124, 126

Sex, 163

Shadow, 153

Shai, 77, 78, 85

Shedy, 27, 42, 158

Shen, 153

Sheps, 38

Shetai, 30

Shetaut Neter, 4, 10, 25, 26, 27, 28, 30, 32, 33, 35, 36, 38, 40, 41, 42, 43, 164

Shetaut Neter See also Egyptian Religion, 4, 10, 25, 26, 27, 28, 30, 32, 33, 35, 36, 38, 40, 41, 42, 43, 164

Shu (air and space), 34, 35, 48, 57, 68, 82

Sirius, 164

Sivananda, Swami, 132

Slave Trade, 101

Sleep, 22

Sleeping Patterns, Sleep, 22

Sma, 41

Smai, 27, 41

Soul, 11, 21, 26, 29, 86, 100, 106, 153, 154

Sphinx, 27, 124

Spirit, 18, 34, 67, 72, 90, 106, 114, 124, 129, 135, 140, 152, 153, 154

Spiritual discipline, 161

Spiritual Preceptor, 4, 66, 70, 71, 73, 104

Spirituality, 160

Study, 42, 119

Sublimation, 163

Sufi, 104

Sufi, see also Sufism, 104

sun, 53, 56, 61, 72, 97, 109

Sun, 53, 56, 61, 72, 97, 109

Sundisk, 45, 121, 123, 140

Sunlight, 153

# GLOSSARY

**AIEMHETEP; IMHOTEP; ASCLEPIUS(Greek):** Celebrated physician of Memphis. Builder of the first pyramid. Deified as a god of medicine and surgery.

**AMENTA:** Underworld; where souls who have passed on from the earthly plane traverse and are judged as to their virtue.

**AMI-UT:** Dweller of the embalmment chamber, a title of ANUBIS.(see ANUBIS).

**APIABU:** "counter of hearts", a name of ANUBIS.(see ANUBIS)

**BENU:** The Phoenix who, upon incineration, rises renewed from the ashes.

**FATHER-MOTHER CREATOR GOD:** The originator, maker of all things, the one called by many names in many religions as the only one; the essence of everything; the Great Spirit,

**DAIMONS:** Administrators of the Gods who carry out duties in the lower spheres of existence. "the duty of the daemons is to give requital." through "good" or "bad" activity since a Daemon's job is activity on behalf of the Gods.

**FACE:** Unmanifest True divine essence of the being achieved through spiritual growth.

**GNOSIS:** Experiential knowledge of the transcendent/divine. see Knowing below.

**GODS:** Advanced souls with great capabilities to carry out the work of the Creator. Children created by the Creator. What wise humans aspire to be.

**HEKAU:** Words of Power

**HORUS:** The brother/nephew of SETHAN, restorer of truth and justice(MAAT).

**IN THE HORIZON:** Subtle realm over which Asar has influence and power to grant life to the dead from our physical realm.

**ASET, AUSET, AST:** Goddess of motherhood, nurturing. Mother of HORUS, dweller in Sothis., resurrector of Asar.

**KHEPERA:** The God represented by the Nile scarab, ever transforming from season to season, coming into the light, as we, engaged in the cycle of rebirth, ever transform from death to life again.

**KMT:** (Pronounced Kamit or Kemet) Ancient name of Egypt as named by its indigenous inhabitants, the Africans later called Hamitic (Black skinned) peoples by Asians(People from the area now called Arabia, Iraq, Iran, etc.) and Eurasians(Greeks, Romans, French, English, etc.). The Black Land, Land of Blackness; Primordial Blackness, Opaqueness, from which all comes(creation); Land of the Black people. Foremost is Asar, redeemer, bestower of everlasting life, He is known as "THE GREAT BLACK"

**KNOWING:** Having information and Having knowledge are not necessarily the same thing. Much in the WORLD is information we are told, much is information gathered by our senses which are made to gather information from the physical realm only.

Since human senses are designed to perceive physical objects, they miss a whole other reality which lies beyond. The "Absolute Truth" or God which underlies all things in the "physical" realm cannot be sensed with the ordinary senses which are designed only for the world of duality.

he universe of male - female, ying - yang, up - down, came from the real of homogeneity, grayness, timelessness, ottomlessness, boundlessness, etc. All limitations of the physical realm came from the limitless realm of the Spirit. his is made perfectly clear in the earliest Cosmogenical scriptures.

herefore, human senses, which are created and exist in the physical universe will be useless in perceiving the Spirit. he change must be within the mind and heart of the individual. The individual must change into the Spirit in order to ee the Spirit.

**LOGOS:** Sermon; discourse; reason; The word; uttered by god which created and maintains creation; universal truth.

**LONG LIVED:** Herein refers to longevity in the spiritual realm, not the physical-temporal.

**MAAT:** Truth, Justice, correctness, righteousness; which cannot be separated from both it's doing and it's speaking. If one does not do *MAAT*, one cannot speak it and vise versa.

**MER:** Pyramid, House of Fire

**MIN:** The god of fertility, and strength of will depicted with erect phallus showing vitality and a raised flail to control t in wisdom .

**NAMES:** The Egyptian language is that of power; not words, sounds fulfilled with deeds, the very Power of the Egyptian Names, have in themselves the Power to bring into act what is said.

**NETER:** God principle, divine manifestation, divine entity assisting the Creator in the management of creation.

**NETERS:** (Divine causal principals-Gods and God's aspects-forces which operate within creation)

**NETERU:** Gods: divine powers latent within humans, divine ways.

**ASAR (ASAR, AUSAR, ASR):** The god of eternal life and reincarnation. The goal state of the seeker of self and godhood through knowledge and wisdom. The title "AUSAR" is given to the successful initiates into the light of self knowledge.

## PARTS OF THE SOUL-SPIRIT
**(1) The KA:** The abstract personality, ethereal body possessing power of locomotion.
**(2) THE KHAT:** The concrete personality, the physical body.
**(3) THE BA:** The heart-soul which dwells in the KA with power of metamorphosis.
**(4) THE AB:** Heart, the animal life in man, rational, spiritual, ethical, undergoes examination by Asar in the Book of Coming forth by day.
**(5) THE KHAIBIT:** Shadow, associated with the BA from whom it receives nourishment and has power of locomotion and omnipresence.
**(6) THE KHU:** Spiritual Soul, which is immortal; associated with the BA and is an Ethereal Being.
**(7) THE SAHU:** Spiritual body in which the KHU dwells; The spiritual and mental attributes of the natural body are united to the new powers of it's own nature.
**(8) THE SEKHEM:** Power; spiritual personification of the vital force in man and woman; It's dwelling place is in the heavens with the KHUS.
**(9) THE REN:** The name; essential attribute to the personification of a being; The name sometimes found encircled by a rope of light called a cartouche which is also associated with the Shen which is associated with the top part of the Ankh Symbol. A rope of Sunlight or life force harnessed into the form of a circle, the most impregnable structure to protect the name against attack.

**Sanctuary of God; The Temple not made with hands; Temple of the human spirit:** The human body.

**SEKHEM OR SHEKEM:** Power, complete control will to manifest what is desired.

**SETHAN:** The God who was originally good and later turned to evil, becoming the precursor of "SATAN", "CAIN" and the modern "DEVIL".

**Sucha Daudi:** Come forth Djehuty; come forth wisdom; into my Soul Spirit, that I may do the will of God, the Supreme Being on Earth.

**TA-MERRY:** Ancient name of Egypt as named by its indigenous inhabitants, the Afrikans later called Hamitic(Black skinned) peoples by Asians(People from the area now called Arabia, Iraq, Iran, etc.) and Eurasians(Greeks, Romans, French, English, etc.).

**TEMT TCHAAS:** a collection or book of sayings containing the primeval wisdom of ancient times.

**THE GOOD:** God, Supreme Being, The All.

**TITAN:** Rulers of the earthly world order; government, social, religious etc. leaders.

**TYPHON:** is the passionate, titanic, reasonless and impulsive aspect of the soul, while of the corporeal side, the death dealing, pestilent and disturbing, with reasonable times.

**VIRTUE:** Any actions that are beneficial to ones self, the family, society, the world and to the universe.

# Bibliography

Original Hieroglyphic Text of the story of Hetheru and Djehuty from the Tomb of Seti I

## Video Lecture Presentation by Sebai Dr. Muata Ashby

The Glorious Light meditation Hieroglyphic Script Part 1
The Glorious Light meditation Hieroglyphic Script Part 2
The Glorious Light meditation Hieroglyphic Script Part 3
The Glorious Light meditation Hieroglyphic Script Part 4

## Music and Guided Meditation Audio Recording for Practicing the Glorious Light Meditation

Track 1 The Glorious Light
Track 2 The Glorious Light Music for Meditation [Instrumental]
Track 3 The Glorious Light Guided Meditation session

www.Egyptianyoga.com

# All Hieroglyphic text and graphics available through the Scribesoft Collection for the PC, designed by Muata Ashby
# SEMA INSTITUTE

Cruzian Mystic P.O.Box 570459, Miami, Florida. 33257 (305) 378-6253, Fax. (305) 378-6253

# Become a Practitioner of the Glorious Light Meditation through Expert Instruction

Learn about teachers in your area. If there are no teachers in your area contact us and earn where instruction will be given or arrange a seminar in your city or country.

Glorious Light Meditation

*Learn to Practice*

Discover and Learn the Special meditation teaching from an original ancient Kemetic text discovered and translated by Sebai Dr. Muata Ashby

*Do it for you...*

It promotes enlightened super consciousness, dynamic mind power, self-mastery, inner peace and vibrant health.

Based on the book

GLORIOUS LIGHT MEDITATION

The Sema Institute
Kemet University

www.Egyptianyoga.com        (305) 305-378-6253
www.Kemetuniversity.com     kemetuniversity@aol.com    In the UK call 011 44 208 800 2727

For More information or to schedule a seminar in your city or country:
www.GloriousLightMeditation.org
www.Egyptianyoga.com
(305)-378-6253 **(305) 378-6253, Fax. (305) 378-6253**

# Become a Certified Kemetic Meditation Instructor

Know Thyself

*"Meditation is the pathway to Self-Mastery and Enlightenment."*
*—Sebai Muata Ashby*

*Uaa Shedy*
## "KEMETIC MEDITATION DISCIPLINE"

**Meditation is the means** to confront the lower self and discover the greatness and best in yourself and in the world. The Neterian Sages of ancient Kamit discovered, over 12,000 years ago the secrets of life and these are now available for all to discover and use to truly reach the fullest potential of life; to discover inner peace, strength of will and fortitude to succeed, supreme mental health and the highest goal, spiritual freedom. They developed five major forms of meditation practice. The Glorious Light System is one of them.

**Practitioner Course:** Attend the upcoming weekend seminar to learn the history, philosophy and technique of Kemetic Meditation.

**Teacher Certification Course:** Attend the upcoming weekend seminar to learn how to practice and teach the practice of Kemetic Meditation.

For More information or to schedule a seminar in your city or country:
www.GloriousLightMeditation.org
www.Egyptianyoga.com
(305)-378-6253

# Glorious Light Meditation
## Teacher Certification Program

Learn and become a teacher of the Special meditation teaching from an original ancient Kemetic text discovered and translated by Sebai Dr. Muata Ashby that promotes enlightened super consciousness, dynamic mind power, self-mastery, inner peace and vibrant health.

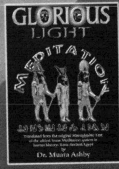

Based on
the book by Sebai Muata Ashby

PRESENTED and TAUGHT
by Sebai Dr. Muata Ashby
and instructors trained
by Dr. Ashby

The Sema Institute
Temple of Shetaut Neter
Kemet University

www.Egyptianyoga.com        (305) 305-378-6253
www.Kemetuniversity.com    kemetuniversity@aol.com    In the UK call 011 44 208 800 2727

# Other Books From C M Books

P.O.Box 570459
Miami, Florida, 33257
(305) 378-6253 Fax: (305) 378-6253

This book is part of a series on the study and practice of Ancient Egyptian Yoga and Mystical Spirituality based on the writings of Dr. Muata Abhaya Ashby. They are also part of the Egyptian Yoga Course provided by the Sema Institute of Yoga. Below you will find a listing of the other books in this series. For more information send for the Egyptian Yoga Book-Audio-Video Catalog or the Egyptian Yoga Course Catalog.

Now you can study the teachings of Egyptian and Indian Yoga wisdom and Spirituality with the Egyptian Yoga Mystical Spirituality Series. The Egyptian Yoga Series takes you through the Initiation process and lead you to understand the mysteries of the soul and the Divine and to attain the highest goal of life: ENLIGHTENMENT. The **Egyptian Yoga Series**, takes you on an in depth study of Ancient Egyptian mythology and their inner mystical meaning. Each Book is prepared for the serious student of the mystical sciences and provides a study of the teachings along with exercises, assignments and projects to make the teachings understood and effective in real life. The Series is part of the Egyptian Yoga course but may be purchased even if you are not taking the course. The series is ideal for study groups.

Prices subject to change.

1. *EGYPTIAN YOGA: THE PHILOSOPHY OF ENLIGHTENMENT* An original, fully illustrated work, including hieroglyphs, detailing the meaning of the Egyptian mysteries, tantric yoga, psycho-spiritual and physical exercises. Egyptian Yoga is a guide to the practice of the highest spiritual philosophy which leads to absolute freedom from human misery and to immortality. It is well known by scholars that Egyptian philosophy is the basis of Western and Middle Eastern religious philosophies such as *Christianity, Islam, Judaism,* the *Kabala,* and Greek philosophy, but what about Indian philosophy, Yoga and Taoism? What were the original teachings? How can they be practiced today? What is the source of pain and suffering in the world and what is the solution? Discover the deepest mysteries of the mind and universe within and outside of your self. 8.5" X 11" ISBN: 1-884564-01-1 Soft $19.95

2. *EGYPTIAN YOGA: African Religion Volume 2-* Theban Theology U.S. In this long awaited sequel to *Egyptian Yoga: The Philosophy of Enlightenment* you will take a fascinating and enlightening journey back in time and discover the teachings which constituted the epitome of Ancient Egyptian spiritual wisdom. What are the disciplines which lead to the fulfillment of all desires? Delve into the three states of consciousness (waking, dream and deep sleep) and the fourth state which transcends them all, Neberdjer, "The Absolute." These teachings of the city of Waset (Thebes) were the crowning achievement of the Sages of Ancient Egypt. They establish the standard mystical keys for understanding the profound mystical symbolism of the Triad of human consciousness. ISBN 1-884564-39-9 $23.95

3. *THE KEMETIC DIET: GUIDE TO HEALTH, DIET AND FASTING* Health issues have always been important to human beings since the beginning of time. The earliest records of history show that the art of healing was held in high esteem since the time of Ancient Egypt. In the early 20th century, medical doctors

160

had almost attained the status of sainthood by the promotion of the idea that they alone were "scientists" while other healing modalities and traditional healers who did not follow the "scientific method' were nothing but superstitious, ignorant charlatans who at best would take the money of their clients and at worst kill them with the unscientific "snake oils" and "irrational theories". In the late 20th century, the failure of the modern medical establishment's ability to lead the general public to good health, promoted the move by many in society towards "alternative medicine". Alternative medicine disciplines are those healing modalities which do not adhere to the philosophy of allopathic medicine. Allopathic medicine is what medical doctors practice by an large. It is the theory that disease is caused by agencies outside the body such as bacteria, viruses or physical means which affect the body. These can therefore be treated by medicines and therapies The natural healing method began in the absence of extensive technologies with the idea that all the answers for health may be found in nature or rather, the deviation from nature. Therefore, the health of the body can be restored by correcting the aberration and thereby restoring balance. This is the area that will be covered in this volume. Allopathic techniques have their place in the art of healing. However, we should not forget that the body is a grand achievement of the spirit and built into it is the capacity to maintain itself and heal itself. Ashby, Muata ISBN: 1-884564-49-6          $28.95

4. INITIATION INTO EGYPTIAN YOGA Shedy: Spiritual discipline or program, to go deeply into the mysteries, to study the mystery teachings and literature profoundly, to penetrate the mysteries. You will learn about the mysteries of initiation into the teachings and practice of Yoga and how to become an Initiate of the mystical sciences. This insightful manual is the first in a series which introduces you to the goals of daily spiritual and yoga practices: Meditation, Diet, Words of Power and the ancient wisdom teachings.  8.5" X 11" ISBN 1-884564-02-X   Soft Cover $24.95  U.S.

5. *THE AFRICAN ORIGINS OF CIVILIZATION, RELIGION AND YOGA SPIRITUALITY AND ETHICS PHILOSOPHY* HARD COVER EDITION Part 1, Part 2, Part 3 in one volume 683 Pages Hard Cover First Edition Three volumes in one. Over the past several years I have been asked to put together in one volume the most important evidences showing the correlations and common teachings between Kamitan (Ancient Egyptian) culture and religion and that of India. The questions of the history of Ancient Egypt, and the latest archeological evidences showing civilization and culture in Ancient Egypt and its spread to other countries, has intrigued many scholars as well as mystics over the years. Also, the possibility that Ancient Egyptian Priests and Priestesses migrated to Greece, India and other countries to carry on the traditions of the Ancient Egyptian Mysteries, has been speculated over the years as well. In chapter 1 of the book *Egyptian Yoga The Philosophy of Enlightenment,* 1995, I first introduced the deepest comparison between Ancient Egypt and India that had been brought forth up to that time. Now, in the year 2001 this new book, *THE AFRICAN ORIGINS OF CIVILIZATION, MYSTICAL RELIGION AND YOGA PHILOSOPHY,* more fully explores the motifs, symbols and philosophical correlations between Ancient Egyptian and Indian mysticism and clearly shows not only that Ancient Egypt and India were connected culturally but also spiritually. How does this knowledge help the spiritual aspirant? This discovery has great importance for the Yogis and mystics who follow the philosophy of Ancient Egypt and the mysticism of India. It means that India has a longer history and heritage than was previously understood. It shows that the mysteries of Ancient Egypt were essentially a yoga tradition which did not die but rather developed into the modern day systems of Yoga technology of India. It further shows that African culture developed Yoga Mysticism earlier than any other civilization in history. All of this expands our understanding of the unity of culture and the deep legacy of Yoga, which stretches into the distant past, beyond the Indus Valley civilization, the earliest known high culture in India as well as the Vedic tradition of Aryan culture. Therefore, Yoga culture and mysticism is the oldest known tradition of spiritual development and Indian mysticism is an extension of the Ancient Egyptian mysticism. By understanding the legacy which Ancient Egypt gave to India the mysticism of India is better understood and by comprehending the heritage of Indian Yoga, which is rooted in Ancient Egypt the Mysticism of Ancient Egypt is also better understood. This expanded understanding allows us to prove the underlying kinship of humanity, through the common symbols, motifs and philosophies which are not disparate and confusing teachings but in reality expressions of the same study of truth through metaphysics and mystical realization of Self. (HARD COVER) ISBN: 1-884564-50-X   $45.00 U.S.   81/2" X 11"

6. *AFRICAN ORIGINS BOOK 1 PART 1* African Origins of African Civilization, Religion, Yoga Mysticism and Ethics Philosophy-Soft Cover $24.95 ISBN: 1-884564-55-0

7. *AFRICAN ORIGINS BOOK 2 PART 2* African Origins of Western Civilization, Religion and Philosophy (Soft) -Soft Cover $24.95 ISBN: 1-884564-56-9

8. *EGYPT AND INDIA AFRICAN ORIGINS OF Eastern Civilization, Religion, Yoga Mysticism and Philosophy*-Soft Cover In chapter 1 of the book *Egyptian Yoga The Philosophy of Enlightenment*, 1995, I first introduced the comparison between spiritual teachings and symbols of Ancient Egypt and India that had been brought forth up to that time. Now, this book, *EGYPT AND INDIA*, more fully explores the motifs, symbols and philosophical correlations between Ancient Egyptian and Indian mysticism and clearly shows not only that Ancient Egypt and India were connected culturally but also spiritually. This book presents evidences like the discovery of the "OM" symbol in Ancient Egyptian texts. How does this knowledge help the spiritual aspirant? This discovery has great importance for the Yogis and mystics who follow the philosophy of Ancient Egypt and the mysticism of India. It means that India has a longer history and heritage than was previously understood. It shows that the mysteries of Ancient Egypt were essentially a yoga tradition which did not die but rather developed into the modern day systems of Yoga technology of India. It further shows that African culture developed Yoga Mysticism earlier than any other civilization in history. All of this expands our understanding of the unity of culture and the deep legacy of Yoga, which stretches into the distant past, beyond the Indus Valley civilization, the earliest known high culture in India as well as the Vedic tradition of Aryan culture. Therefore, Yoga culture and mysticism is the oldest known tradition of spiritual development and Indian mysticism is an extension of the Ancient Egyptian mysticism. By understanding the legacy which Ancient Egypt gave to India the mysticism of India is better understood and by comprehending the heritage of Indian Yoga, which is rooted in Ancient Egypt the Mysticism of Ancient Egypt is also better understood. This expanded understanding allows us to prove the underlying kinship of humanity, through the common symbols, motifs and philosophies which are not disparate and confusing teachings but in reality expressions of the same study of truth through metaphysics and mystical realization of Self. **$29.95 (Soft) ISBN: 1-884564-57-7**

9. *THE MYSTERIES OF ISIS:* **The Ancient Egyptian Philosophy of Self-Realization** - There are several paths to discover the Divine and the mysteries of the higher Self. This volume details the mystery teachings of the goddess Aset (Isis) from Ancient Egypt- the path of wisdom. It includes the teachings of her temple and the disciplines that are enjoined for the initiates of the temple of Aset as they were given in ancient times. Also, this book includes the teachings of the main myths of Aset that lead a human being to spiritual enlightenment and immortality. Through the study of ancient myth and the illumination of initiatic understanding the idea of God is expanded from the mythological comprehension to the metaphysical. Then this metaphysical understanding is related to you, the student, so as to begin understanding your true divine nature. ISBN 1-884564-24-0 $22.99

10. *EGYPTIAN PROVERBS:* collection of —Ancient Egyptian Proverbs and Wisdom Teachings -How to live according to MAAT Philosophy. Beginning Meditation. All proverbs are indexed for easy searches. For the first time in one volume, ——Ancient Egyptian Proverbs, wisdom teachings and meditations, fully illustrated with hieroglyphic text and symbols. EGYPTIAN PROVERBS is a unique collection of knowledge and wisdom which you can put into practice today and transform your life. $14.95 U.S        ISBN: 1-884564-00-3

11. *GOD OF LOVE: THE PATH OF DIVINE LOVE The Process of Mystical Transformation and The Path of Divine Love*        This Volume focuses on the ancient wisdom teachings of "Neter Merri" –the Ancient Egyptian philosophy of Divine Love and how to use them in a scientific process for self-transformation. Love is one of the most powerful human emotions. It is also the source of Divine feeling that unifies God and the individual human being. When love is fragmented and diminished by egoism the Divine connection is lost. The Ancient tradition of Neter Merri leads human beings back to their Divine connection, allowing them to discover their innate glorious self that is actually Divine and immortal. This volume will detail the process of transformation from ordinary consciousness to cosmic consciousness through the integrated practice of the teachings and the path of Devotional Love toward the Divine. 5.5"x 8.5" ISBN 1-884564-11-9  $22.95

12. *INTRODUCTION TO MAAT PHILOSOPHY: Spiritual Enlightenment Through the Path of Virtue*  Known commonly as Karma in India, the teachings of MAAT contain an extensive philosophy based on ariu (deeds)

and their fructification in the form of shai and renenet (fortune and destiny, leading to Meskhenet (fate in a future birth) for living virtuously and with orderly wisdom are explained and the student is to begin practicing the precepts of Maat in daily life so as to promote the process of purification of the heart in preparation for the judgment of the soul. This judgment will be understood not as an event that will occur at the time of death but as an event that occurs continuously, at every moment in the life of the individual. The student will learn how to become allied with the forces of the Higher Self and to thereby begin cleansing the mind (heart) of impurities so as to attain a higher vision of reality. ISBN 1-884564-20-8  $22.99

3.     *MEDITATION The Ancient Egyptian Path to Enlightenment*     Many people do not know about the rich history of meditation practice in Ancient Egypt. This volume outlines the theory of meditation and presents the Ancient Egyptian Hieroglyphic text which give instruction as to the nature of the mind and its three modes of expression. It also presents the texts which give instruction on the practice of meditation for spiritual Enlightenment and unity with the Divine. This volume allows the reader to begin practicing meditation by explaining, in easy to understand terms, the simplest form of meditation and working up to the most advanced form which was practiced in ancient times and which is still practiced by yogis around the world in modern times. ISBN 1-884564-27-7  $22.99

14.     *THE GLORIOUS LIGHT MEDITATION* TECHNIQUE OF ANCIENT EGYPT New for the year 2000. This volume is based on the earliest known instruction in history given for the practice of formal meditation. Discovered by Dr. Muata Ashby, it is inscribed on the walls of the Tomb of Seti I in Thebes Egypt. This volume details the philosophy and practice of this unique system of meditation originated in Ancient Egypt and the earliest practice of meditation known in the world which occurred in the most advanced African Culture. ISBN: 1-884564-15-1 $16.95 (PB)

15.     *THE SERPENT POWER: The Ancient Egyptian Mystical Wisdom of the Inner Life Force.*     This Volume specifically deals with the latent life Force energy of the universe and in the human body, its control and sublimation. How to develop the Life Force energy of the subtle body. This Volume will introduce the esoteric wisdom of the science of how virtuous living acts in a subtle and mysterious way to cleanse the latent psychic energy conduits and vortices of the spiritual body. ISBN 1-884564-19-4  $22.95

16.     *EGYPTIAN YOGA The Postures of The Gods and Goddesses* Discover the physical postures and exercises practiced thousands of years ago in Ancient Egypt which are today known as Yoga exercises. Discover the history of the postures and how they were transferred from Ancient Egypt in Africa to India through Buddhist Tantrism. Then practice the postures as you discover the mythic teaching that originally gave birth to the postures and was practiced by the Ancient Egyptian priests and priestesses. This work is based on the pictures and teachings from the Creation story of Ra, The Asarian Resurrection Myth and the carvings and reliefs from various Temples in Ancient Egypt 8.5" X 11" ISBN 1-884564-10-0  Soft Cover $21.95      Exercise video  $20

17.     *SACRED SEXUALITY: EGYPTIAN TANTRA YOGA:*     *The Art of Sex* Sublimation and Universal Consciousness This Volume will expand on the male and female principles within the human body and in the universe and further detail the sublimation of sexual energy into spiritual energy. The student will study the deities Min and Hathor, Asar and Aset, Geb and Nut and discover the mystical implications for a practical spiritual discipline. This Volume will also focus on the Tantric aspects of Ancient Egyptian and Indian mysticism, the purpose of sex and the mystical teachings of sexual sublimation which lead to self-knowledge and Enlightenment. 5.5"x 8.5"  ISBN 1-884564-03-8     $24.95

18.     *AFRICAN RELIGION Volume 4: ASARIAN THEOLOGY: RESURRECTING OSIRIS* The path of Mystical Awakening and the Keys to Immortality NEW REVISED AND EXPANDED EDITION!     The Ancient Sages created stories based on human and superhuman beings whose struggles, aspirations, needs and desires ultimately lead them to discover their true Self. The myth of Aset, Asar and Heru is no exception in this area. While there is no one source where the entire story may be found, pieces of it are inscribed in various ancient Temples walls, tombs, steles and papyri.  For the first time available, the complete myth of Asar, Aset and Heru has been compiled from original Ancient Egyptian, Greek and Coptic Texts. This epic myth has been richly illustrated with reliefs from the Temple of Heru at Edfu, the Temple of Aset at Philae, the Temple of

Asar at Abydos, the Temple of Hathor at Denderah and various papyri, inscriptions and reliefs. Discover the myth which inspired the teachings of the *Shetaut Neter* (Egyptian Mystery System - Egyptian Yoga) and the Egyptian Book of Coming Forth By Day. Also, discover the three levels of Ancient Egyptian Religion, how to understand the mysteries of the Duat or Astral World and how to discover the abode of the Supreme in the Amenta, *The Other World*   The ancient religion of Asar, Aset and Heru, if properly understood, contains all of the elements necessary to lead the sincere aspirant to attain immortality through inner self-discovery. This volume presents the entire myth and explores the main mystical themes and rituals associated with the myth for understating human existence, creation and the way to achieve spiritual emancipation - *Resurrection.* The Asarian myth is so powerful that it influenced and is still having an effect on the major world religions. Discover the origins and mystical meaning of the Christian Trinity, the Eucharist ritual and the ancient origin of the birthday of Jesus Christ. Soft Cover ISBN: 1-884564-27-5 $24.95

19.  *THE EGYPTIAN BOOK OF THE DEAD MYSTICISM OF THE PERT EM HERU* " I Know myself, I know myself, I am One With God!–From the Pert Em Heru "The Ru Pert em Heru" or "Ancient Egyptian Book of The Dead," or "Book of Coming Forth By Day" as it is more popularly known, has fascinated the world since the successful translation of Ancient Egyptian hieroglyphic scripture over 150 years ago. The astonishing writings in it reveal that the Ancient Egyptians believed in life after death and in an ultimate destiny to discover the Divine. The elegance and aesthetic beauty of the hieroglyphic text itself has inspired many see it as an art form in and of itself. But is there more to it than that? Did the Ancient Egyptian wisdom contain more than just aphorisms and hopes of eternal life beyond death? In this volume Dr. Muata Ashby, the author of over 25 books on Ancient Egyptian Yoga Philosophy has produced a new translation of the original texts which uncovers a mystical teaching underlying the sayings and rituals instituted by the Ancient Egyptian Sages and Saints. "Once the philosophy of Ancient Egypt is understood as a mystical tradition instead of as a religion or primitive mythology, it reveals its secrets which if practiced today will lead anyone to discover the glory of spiritual self-discovery. The Pert em Heru is in every way comparable to the Indian Upanishads or the Tibetan Book of the Dead." □ $28.95    ISBN# 1-884564-28-3 Size: 8½" X 11

20.  *African Religion VOL. 1- ANUNIAN THEOLOGY THE MYSTERIES OF RA* The Philosophy of Anu and The Mystical Teachings of The Ancient Egyptian  Creation Myth Discover the mystical teachings contained in the Creation Myth and the gods and goddesses who brought creation and human beings into existence. The Creation myth of Anu is the source of Anunian Theology but also of the other main theological systems of Ancient Egypt that also influenced other world religions including Christianity, Hinduism and Buddhism. The Creation Myth holds the key to understanding the universe and for attaining spiritual Enlightenment. ISBN: 1-884564-38-0 $19.95

21.  *African Religion VOL  3: Memphite Theology: MYSTERIES OF MIND* Mystical Psychology & Mental Health for Enlightenment and Immortality based on the Ancient Egyptian Philosophy of Menefer -Mysticism of Ptah, Egyptian Physics and Yoga Metaphysics and the Hidden properties of Matter.    This volume uncovers the mystical psychology of the Ancient Egyptian wisdom teachings centering on the philosophy of the Ancient Egyptian city of Menefer (Memphite Theology). How to understand the mind and how to control the senses and lead the mind to health, clarity and mystical self-discovery. This Volume will also go deeper into the philosophy of God as creation and will explore the concepts of modern science and how they correlate with ancient teachings. This Volume will lay the ground work for the understanding of the philosophy of universal consciousness and the initiatic/yogic insight into who or what is God? ISBN 1-884564-07-0   $22.95

22.  *AFRICAN RELIGION VOLUME 5: THE GODDESS AND THE EGYPTIAN MYSTERIESTHE PATH OF THE GODDESS THE GODDESS PATH* The Secret Forms of the Goddess and the Rituals of Resurrection The Supreme Being may be worshipped as father or as mother. *Ushet Rekhat* or *Mother Worship*, is the spiritual process of worshipping the Divine in the form of the Divine Goddess. It celebrates the most important forms of the Goddess including *Nathor, Maat, Aset, Arat, Amentet and Hathor* and explores their mystical meaning as well as the rising of *Sirius,* the star of  Aset (Aset) and the new birth of Hor (Heru). The end of the year is a time of reckoning, reflection and engendering a new or renewed positive movement toward attaining spiritual Enlightenment. The Mother Worship devotional meditation ritual, performed on five days during the month of December and on New Year's Eve, is based on the Ushet Rekhit. During the

ceremony, the cosmic forces, symbolized by Sirius - and the constellation of Orion ---, are harnessed through the understanding and devotional attitude of the participant. This propitiation draws the light of wisdom and health to all those who share in the ritual, leading to prosperity and wisdom. $14.95 ISBN 1-884564-18-6

23. *THE MYSTICAL JOURNEY FROM JESUS TO CHRIST* Discover the ancient Egyptian origins of Christianity before the Catholic Church and learn the mystical teachings given by Jesus to assist all humanity in becoming Christlike. Discover the secret meaning of the Gospels that were discovered in Egypt. Also discover how and why so many Christian churches came into being. Discover that the Bible still holds the keys to mystical realization even though its original writings were changed by the church. Discover how to practice the original teachings of Christianity which leads to the Kingdom of Heaven. $24.95      ISBN# 1-884564-05-4 size: 8½" X 11"

24. *THE STORY OF ASAR, ASET AND HERU:* An Ancient Egyptian Legend (For Children)    Now for the first time, the most ancient myth of Ancient Egypt comes alive for children. Inspired by the books *The Asarian Resurrection: The Ancient Egyptian Bible* and *The Mystical Teachings of The Asarian Resurrection, The Story of Asar, Aset and Heru* is an easy to understand and thrilling tale which inspired the children of Ancient Egypt to aspire to greatness and righteousness.   If you and your child have enjoyed stories like *The Lion King* and *Star Wars you will love The Story of Asar, Aset and Heru.* Also, if you know the story of Jesus and Krishna you will discover than Ancient Egypt had a similar myth and that this myth carries important spiritual teachings for living a fruitful and fulfilling life. This book may be used along with *The Parents Guide To The Asarian Resurrection Myth: How to Teach Yourself and Your Child the Principles of Universal Mystical Religion.* The guide provides some background to the Asarian Resurrection myth and it also gives insight into the mystical teachings contained in it which you may introduce to your child. It is designed for parents who wish to grow spiritually with their children and it serves as an introduction for those who would like to study the Asarian Resurrection Myth in depth and to practice its teachings. 8.5" X 11"     ISBN: 1-884564-31-3   $12.95

25. *THE PARENTS GUIDE TO THE AUSARIAN RESURRECTION MYTH:*  How to Teach Yourself and Your Child  the Principles of Universal Mystical Religion.   This insightful manual brings for the timeless wisdom of the ancient through the Ancient Egyptian myth of Asar, Aset and Heru and the mystical teachings contained in it for parents who want to guide their children to understand and practice the teachings of mystical spirituality. This manual may be used with the children's storybook *The Story of Asar, Aset and Heru* by Dr. Muata Abhaya Ashby.    ISBN: 1-884564-30-5   $16.95

26. *HEALING THE CRIMINAL HEART.* Introduction to Maat Philosophy, Yoga and Spiritual Redemption Through the Path of Virtue    Who is a criminal? Is there such a thing as a criminal heart? What is the source of evil and sinfulness and is there any way to rise above it? Is there redemption for those who have committed sins, even the worst crimes?    Ancient Egyptian mystical psychology holds important answers to these questions. Over ten thousand years ago mystical psychologists, the Sages of Ancient Egypt, studied and charted the human mind and spirit and laid out a path which will lead to spiritual redemption, prosperity and Enlightenment.    This introductory volume brings forth the teachings of the Asarian Resurrection, the most important myth of Ancient Egypt, with relation to the faults of human existence: anger, hatred, greed, lust, animosity, discontent, ignorance, egoism jealousy, bitterness, and a myriad of psycho-spiritual ailments which keep a human being in a state of negativity and adversity    ISBN: 1-884564-17-8   $15.95

27. *TEMPLE RITUAL OF THE ANCIENT EGYPTIAN MYSTERIES--THEATER & DRAMA OF THE ANCIENT EGYPTIAN MYSTERIES*: Details the practice of the mysteries and ritual program of the temple and the philosophy an practice of the ritual of the mysteries, its purpose and execution. Featuring the Ancient Egyptian stage play-"The Enlightenment of Hathor' Based on an Ancient Egyptian Drama, The original Theater -Mysticism of the Temple of Hetheru 1-884564-14-3  $19.95  By Dr. Muata Ashby

28. *GUIDE TO PRINT ON DEMAND: SELF-PUBLISH FOR PROFIT, SPIRITUAL FULFILLMENT AND SERVICE TO HUMANITY* Everyone asks us how we produced so many books in such a short time. Here are the secrets to writing and producing books that uplift humanity and how to get them printed for a fraction of the regular cost. Anyone can become an author even if they have limited funds. All that is necessary is the willingness to

learn how the printing and book business work and the desire to follow the special instructions given here for preparing your manuscript format. Then you take your work directly to the non-traditional companies who can produce your books for less than the traditional book printer can. ISBN: 1-884564-40-2    $16.95 U. S.

29.   *Egyptian Mysteries: Vol. 1,* Shetaut Neter What are the Mysteries? For thousands of years the spiritual tradition of Ancient Egypt, *Shetaut Neter,* "The Egyptian Mysteries," "The Secret Teachings," have fascinated, tantalized and amazed the world. At one time exalted and recognized as the highest culture of the world, by Africans, Europeans, Asiatics, Hindus, Buddhists and other cultures of the ancient world, in time it was shunned by the emerging orthodox world religions. Its temples desecrated, its philosophy maligned, its tradition spurned, its philosophy dormant in the mystical *Medu Neter,* the mysterious hieroglyphic texts which hold the secret symbolic meaning that has scarcely been discerned up to now. What are the secrets of *Nehast* {spiritual awakening and emancipation, resurrection}. More than just a literal translation, this volume is for awakening to the secret code *Shetitu* of the teaching which was not deciphered by Egyptologists, nor could be understood by ordinary spiritualists. This book is a reinstatement of the original science made available for our times, to the reincarnated followers of Ancient Egyptian culture and the prospect of spiritual freedom to break the bonds of *Khemn,* "ignorance," and slavery to evil forces: *Såaa* . ISBN: 1-884564-41-0 $19.99

30.   *EGYPTIAN MYSTERIES VOL 2:* Dictionary of Gods and Goddesses This book is about the mystery of neteru, the gods and goddesses of Ancient Egypt (Kamit, Kemet). Neteru means "Gods and Goddesses." But the Neterian teaching of Neteru represents more than the usual limited modern day concept of "divinities" or "spirits." The Neteru of Kamit are also metaphors, cosmic principles and vehicles for the enlightening teachings of Shetaut Neter (Ancient Egyptian-African Religion). Actually they are the elements for one of the most advanced systems of spirituality ever conceived in human history. Understanding the concept of neteru provides a firm basis for spiritual evolution and the pathway for viable culture, peace on earth and a healthy human society.     Why is it important to have gods and goddesses in our lives? In order for spiritual evolution to be possible, once a human being has accepted that there is existence after death and there is a transcendental being who exists beyond time and space knowledge, human beings need a connection to that which transcends the ordinary experience of human life in time and space and a means to understand the transcendental reality beyond the mundane reality. ISBN: 1-884564-23-2    $21.95

31.   *EGYPTIAN MYSTERIES VOL. 3* The Priests and Priestesses of Ancient Egypt This volume details the path of Neterian priesthood, the joys, challenges and rewards of advanced Neterian life, the teachings that allowed the priests and priestesses to manage the most long lived civilization in human history and how that path can be adopted today; for those who want to tread the path of the Clergy of Shetaut Neter. ISBN: 1-884564-53-4 $24.95

32.   *The War of Heru and Set:* The Struggle of Good and Evil for Control of the World and The Human Soul This volume contains a novelized version of the Asarian Resurrection myth that is based on the actual scriptures presented in the Book Asarian Religion (old name –Resurrecting Osiris). This volume is prepared in the form of a screenplay and can be easily adapted to be used as a stage play. Spiritual seeking is a mythic journey that has many emotional highs and lows, ecstasies and depressions, victories and frustrations. This is the War of Life that is played out in the myth as the struggle of Heru and Set and those are mythic characters that represent the human Higher and Lower self. How to understand the war and emerge victorious in the journey o life? The ultimate victory and fulfillment can be experienced, which is not changeable or lost in time. The purpose of myth is to convey the wisdom of life through the story of divinities who show the way to overcome the challenges and foibles of life. In this volume the feelings and emotions of the characters of the myth have been highlighted to show the deeply rich texture of the Ancient Egyptian myth. This myth contains deep spiritual teachings and insights into the nature of self, of God and the mysteries of life and the means to discover the true meaning of life and thereby achieve the true purpose of life. To become victorious in the battle of life means to become the King (or Queen) of Egypt.Have you seen movies like The Lion King, Hamlet, The Odyssey, or The Little Buddha? These have been some of the most popular movies in modern times. The Sema Institute of Yoga is dedicated to researching and presenting the wisdom and culture

of ancient Africa. The Script is designed to be produced as a motion picture but may be addapted for the theater as well. $21.95   copyright 1998 By Dr. Muata Ashby ISBN 1-8840564-44-5

3.  *AFRICAN DIONYSUS: FROM EGYPT TO GREECE:* The Kamitan Origins of Greek Culture and Religion ISBN: 1-884564-47-X   FROM EGYPT TO GREECE   This insightful manual is a reference to Ancient Egyptian mythology and philosophy and its correlation to what later became known as Greek and Rome mythology and philosophy. It outlines the basic tenets of the mythologies and shoes the ancient origins of Greek culture in Ancient Egypt. This volume also documents the origins of the Greek alphabet in Egypt as well as Greek religion, myth and philosophy of the gods and goddesses from Egypt from the myth of Atlantis and archaic period with the Minoans to the Classical period. This volume also acts as a resource for Colleges students who would like to set up fraternities and sororities based on the original Ancient Egyptian principles of Sheti and Maat philosophy. ISBN: 1-884564-47-X $22.95 U.S.

34.  *THE FORTY TWO   PRECEPTS OF MAAT,   THE PHILOSOPHY OF   RIGHTEOUS ACTION AND THE ANCIENT EGYPTIAN WISDOM TEXTS ADVANCED STUDIES*   This manual is designed for use with the 1998 Maat Philosophy Class conducted by Dr. Muata Ashby. This is a detailed study of Maat Philosophy. It contains a compilation of the 42 laws or precepts of Maat and the corresponding principles which they represent along with the teachings of the ancient Egyptian Sages relating to each. Maat philosophy was the basis of Ancient Egyptian society and government as well as the heart of Ancient Egyptian myth and spirituality. Maat is at once a goddess, a cosmic force and a living social doctrine, which promotes social harmony and thereby paves the way for spiritual evolution in all levels of society. ISBN: 1-884564-48-8 $16.95 U.S.

35.  **THE SECRET LOTUS: *Poetry of Enlightenment***
Discover the mystical sentiment of the Kemetic teaching as expressed through the poetry of Sebai Muata Ashby. The teaching of spiritual awakening is uniquely experienced when the poetic sensibility is present. This first volume contains the poems written between 1996 and 2003. **1-884564--16 -X  $16.99**

36.  **The Ancient Egyptian Buddha: The Ancient Egyptian Origins of Buddhism**
This book is a compilation of several sections of a larger work, a book by the name of African Origins of Civilization, Religion, Yoga Mysticism and Ethics Philosophy. It also contains some additional evidences not contained in the larger work that demonstrate the correlation between Ancient Egyptian Religion and Buddhism. This book is one of several compiled short volumes that has been compiled so as to facilitate access to specific subjects contained in the larger work which is over 680 pages long. These short and small volumes have been specifically designed to cover one subject in a brief and low cost format. This present volume, The Ancient Egyptian Buddha: The Ancient Egyptian Origins of Buddhism, formed one subject in the larger work; actually it was one chapter of the larger work. However, this volume has some new additional evidences and comparisons of Buddhist and Neterian (Ancient Egyptian) philosophies not previously discussed. It was felt that this subject needed to be discussed because even in the early 21st century, the idea persists that Buddhism originated only in India independently. Yet there is ample evidence from ancient writings and perhaps more importantly, iconographical evidences from the Ancient Egyptians and early Buddhists themselves that prove otherwise. This handy volume has been designed to be accessible to young adults and all others who would like to have an easy reference with documentation on this important subject. This is an important subject because the frame of reference with which we look at a culture depends strongly on our conceptions about its origins. in this case, if we look at the Buddhism as an Asiatic religion we would treat it and it's culture in one way. If we id as African [Ancient Egyptian] we not only would see it in a different light but we also must ascribe Africa with a glorious legacy that matches any other culture in human history and gave rise to one of the present day most important religious philosophies. We would also look at the culture and philosophies of the Ancient Egyptians as having African insights that offer us greater depth into the Buddhist philosophies. Those insights inform our knowledge about other African traditions and we can also begin to understand in a deeper way the effect of Ancient Egyptian culture on African culture and also on the Asiatic as well. We would also be able to discover the glorious and wondrous teaching of mystical philosophy that Ancient Egyptian Shetaut Neter religion offers, that is as powerful as any other mystic system of spiritual philosophy in the world today. ISBN: 1-884564-61-5     $28.95

37.  **The Death of American Empire: Neo-conservatism, Theocracy, Economic Imperialism, Environmental Disaster and the Collapse of Civilization**

167

This work is a collection of essays relating to social and economic, leadership, and ethics, ecological and religious issues that are facing the world today in order to understand the course of history that has led humanity to its present condition and then arrive at positive solutions that will lead to better outcomes for all humanity. It surveys the development and decline of major empires throughout history and focuses on the creation of American Empire along with the social, political and economic policies that led to the prominence of the United States of America as a Superpower including the rise of the political control of the neo-con political philosophy including militarism and the military industrial complex in American politics and the rise of the religious right into and American Theocracy movement. This volume details, through historical and current events, the psychology behind the dominance of western culture in world politics through the "Superpower Syndrome Mandatory Conflict Complex" that drives the Superpower culture to establish itself above all others and then act hubristically to dominate world culture through legitimate influences as well as coercion, media censorship and misinformation leading to international hegemony and world conflict. This volume also details the financial policies that gave rise to American prominence in the global economy, especially after World War II, and promoted American preeminence over the world economy through Globalization as well as the environmental policies, including the oil economy, that are promoting degradation of the world ecology and contribute to the decline of America as an Empire culture. This volume finally explores the factors pointing to the decline of the American Empire economy and imperial power and what to expect in the aftermath of American prominence and how to survive the decline while at the same time promoting policies and social-economic-religious-political changes that are needed in order to promote the emergence of a beneficial and sustainable culture. **$25.95soft** 1-884564-25-9, Hard Cover **$29.95soft** 1-884564-45-3

### 38. The African Origins of Hatha Yoga: And its Ancient Mystical Teaching

The subject of this present volume, The Ancient Egyptian Origins of Yoga Postures, formed one subject in the larger works, African Origins of Civilization Religion, Yoga Mysticism and Ethics Philosophy and the Book Egypt and India is the section of the book African Origins of Civilization. Those works contain the collection of all correlations between Ancient Egypt and India. This volume also contains some additional information not contained in the previous work. It was felt that this subject needed to be discussed more directly, being treated in one volume, as opposed to being contained in the larger work along with other subjects, because even in the early 21st century, the idea persists that the Yoga and specifically, Yoga Postures, were invented and developed only in India. The Ancient Egyptians were peoples originally from Africa who were, in ancient times, colonists in India. Therefore it is no surprise that many Indian traditions including religious and Yogic, would be found earlier in Ancient Egypt. Yet there is ample evidence from ancient writings and perhaps more importantly, iconographical evidences from the Ancient Egyptians themselves and the Indians themselves that prove the connection between Ancient Egypt and India as well as the existence of a discipline of Yoga Postures in Ancient Egypt long before its practice in India. This handy volume has been designed to be accessible to young adults and all others who would like to have an easy reference with documentation on this important subject. This is an important subject because the frame of reference with which we look at a culture depends strongly on our conceptions about its origins. In this case, if we look at the Ancient Egyptians as Asiatic peoples we would treat them and their culture in one way. If we see them as Africans we not only see them in a different light but we also must ascribe Africa with a glorious legacy that matches any other culture in human history. We would also look at the culture and philosophies of the Ancient Egyptians as having African insights instead of Asiatic ones. Those insights inform our knowledge bout other African traditions and we can also begin to understand in a deeper way the effect of Ancient Egyptian culture on African culture and also on the Asiatic as well. When we discover the deeper and more ancient practice of the postures system in Ancient Egypt that was called "Hatha Yoga" in India, we are able to find a new and expanded understanding of the practice that constitutes a discipline of spiritual practice that informs and revitalizes the Indian practices as well as all spiritual disciplines. $19.99 ISBN 1-884564-60-7

### 39. The Black Ancient Egyptians

This present volume, The Black Ancient Egyptians: The Black African Ancestry of the Ancient Egyptians, formed one subject in the larger work: The African Origins of Civilization, Religion, Yoga Mysticism and Ethics Philosophy. It was felt that this subject needed to be discussed because even in the early 21st century, the idea persists that the Ancient Egyptians were peoples originally from Asia Minor who came into North-East Africa. Yet there is ample evidence from ancient writings and perhaps more importantly, iconographical evidences from the Ancient Egyptians themselves that proves otherwise. This handy volume has been designed to be accessible to young adults and all others who would like to have an easy reference with documentation on this important subject. This is an important subject because the frame of reference with which we look at a culture depends strongly on our conceptions about its origins.

this case, if we look at the Ancient Egyptians as Asiatic peoples we would treat them and their culture in one way. If e see them as Africans we not only see them in a different light but we also must ascribe Africa with a glorious legacy at matches any other culture in human history. We would also look at the culture and philosophies of the Ancient gyptians as having African insights instead of Asiatic ones. Those insights inform our knowledge bout other African raditions and we can also begin to understand in a deeper way the effect of Ancient Egyptian culture on African ulture and also on the Asiatic as well. ISBN 1-884564-21-6   $19.99

### 40.   The Limits of Faith: The Failure of Faith-based Religions and the Solution to the Meaning of Life

s faith belief in something without proof? And if so is there never to be any proof or discovery? If so what is the need f intellect? If faith is trust in something that is real is that reality historical, literal or metaphorical or philosophical? If nowledge is an essential element in faith why should there by so much emphasis on believing and not on nderstanding in the modern practice of religion? This volume is a compilation of essays related to the nature of eligious faith in the context of its inception in human history as well as its meaning for religious practice and relations etween religions in modern times. Faith has come to be regarded as a virtuous goal in life. However, many people ave asked how can it be that an endeavor that is supposed to be dedicated to spiritual upliftment has led to more onflict in human history than any other social factor? ISBN 1884564631 SOFT COVER - $19.99, ISBN 1884564623 IARD COVER -$28.95

### 41.  Redemption of The Criminal Heart Through Kemetic Spirituality and Maat Philosophy

Special book dedicated to inmates, their families and members of the Law Enforcement community to promote nderstanding of the cause of transgressions and how to resolve those issues so that a human being may rediscover heir humanity and come back to the family of humanity and also regain the capacity to fully engage in positive spiritual evolution. ISBN: 1-884564-70-4

### 42. COMPARATIVE MYTHOLOGY

What are Myth and Culture and what is their importance for understanding the development of societies, human evolution and the search for meaning? What is the purpose of culture and how do cultures evolve? What are the elements of a culture and how can those elements be broken down and the constituent parts of a culture understood and compared? How do cultures interact? How does enculturation occur and how do people interact with other cultures? How do the processes of acculturation and cooptation occur and what does this mean for the development of a society? How can the study of myths and the elements of culture help in understanding the meaning of life and the means to promote understanding and peace in the world of human activity? This volume is the exposition of a method for studying and comparing cultures, myths and other social aspects of a society. It is an expansion on the Cultural Category Factor Correlation method for studying and comparing myths, cultures, religions and other aspects of human culture. It was originally introduced in the year 2002. This volume contains an expanded treatment as well as several refinements along with examples of the application of the method. the apparent. I hope you enjoy these art renditions as serene reflections of the mysteries of life.  ISBN: 1-884564-72-0
Book price $21.95

### 43. CONVERSATION WITH GOD: Revelations of the Important Questions of Life
**$24.99 U.S.**

This volume contains a grouping of some of the questions that have been submitted to Sebai Dr. Muata Ashby. They are efforts by many aspirants to better understand and practice the teachings of mystical spirituality. It is said that when sages are asked spiritual questions they are relaying the wisdom of God, the Goddess, the Higher Self, etc.  There is a very special quality about the Q & A process that does not occur during a regular lecture session. Certain points come out that would not come out otherwise due to the nature of the process which ideally occurs after a lecture. Having been to a certain degree enlightened by a lecture certain new questions arise and the answers to these have the effect of elevating the teaching of the lecture to even higher levels. Therefore, enjoy these exchanges and may they lead you to enlightenment, peace and prosperity.  ISBN: 1-884564-68-2

### 44. MYSTIC ART PAINTINGS

(with Full Color images) This book contains a collection of the small number of paintings that I have created over the years. Some were used as early book covers and others were done simply to express certain spiritual feelings; some were created for no purpose except to express the joy of color and the feeling of relaxed freedom. All are to elicit mystical awakening in the viewer. Writing a book on philosophy is like sculpture, the more the work is rewritten the reflections and ideas become honed and take form and become clearer and imbued with intellectual beauty. Mystic music is like meditation, a world of its own that exists about 1 inch above ground wherein the musician does not touch the ground. Mystic Graphic Art is meditation in form, color, image and reflected image which opens the door to the reality behind the apparent. I hope you enjoy these art renditions and my reflections on them as serene reflections of the mysteries of life, as visual renditions of the philosophy I have written about over the years. ISBN 1-884564-69-( $19.95

## 45. ANCIENT EGYPTIAN HIEROGLYPHS FOR BEGINNERS

This brief guide was prepared for those inquiring about how to enter into Hieroglyphic studies on their own at home or in study groups. First of all you should know that there are a few institutions around the world which teach how to read the Hieroglyphic text but due to the nature of the study there are perhaps only a handful of people who can read fluently. It is possible for anyone with average intelligence to achieve a high level of proficiency in reading inscriptions on temples and artifacts; however, reading extensive texts is another issue entirely. However, this introduction will give you entry into those texts if assisted by dictionaries and other aids. Most Egyptologists have a basic knowledge and keep dictionaries and notes handy when it comes to dealing with more difficult texts. Medtu Neter or the Ancient Egyptian hieroglyphic language has been considered as a "Dead Language." However, dead languages have always been studied by individuals who for the most part have taught themselves through various means. This book will discuss those means and how to use them most efficiently. ISBN 1884564429 **$28.95**

## 46. ON THE MYSTERIES: Wisdom of An Ancient Egyptian Sage -with Foreword by Muata Ashby

This volume, On the Mysteries, by Iamblichus (Abamun) is a unique form or scripture out of the Ancient Egyptian religious tradition. It is written in a form that is not usual or which is not usually found in the remnants of Ancient Egyptian scriptures. It is in the form of teacher and disciple, much like the Eastern scriptures such as Bhagavad Gita or the Upanishads. This form of writing may not have been necessary in Ancient times, because the format of teaching in Egypt was different prior to the conquest period by the Persians, Assyrians, Greeks and later the Romans. The question and answer format can be found but such extensive discourses and corrections of misunderstandings within the context of a teacher - disciple relationship is not usual. It therefore provides extensive insights into the times when it was written and the state of practice of Ancient Egyptian and other mystery religions. This has important implications for our times because we are today, as in the Greco-Roman period, also besieged with varied religions and new age philosophies as well as social strife and war. How can we understand our times and also make sense of the forest of spiritual traditions? How can we cut through the cacophony of religious fanaticism, and ignorance as well as misconceptions about the mysteries on the other in order to discover the true purpose of religion and the secret teachings that open up the mysteries of life and the way to enlightenment and immortality? This book, which comes to us from so long ago, offers us transcendental wisdom that applied to the world two thousand years ago as well as our world today. ISBN 1-884564-64-X    $25.95

## 47. The Ancient Egyptian Wisdom Texts -Compiled by Muata Ashby

The Ancient Egyptian Wisdom Texts are a genre of writings from the ancient culture that have survived to the present and provide a vibrant record of the practice of spiritual evolution otherwise known as religion or yoga philosophy in Ancient Egypt. The principle focus of the Wisdom Texts is the cultivation of understanding, peace, harmony, selfless service, self-control, Inner fulfillment and spiritual realization. When these factors are cultivated in human life, the virtuous qualities in a human being begin to manifest and sinfulness, ignorance and negativity diminish until a person is able to enter into higher consciousness, the coveted goal of all civilizations. It is this virtuous mode of life which opens the door to self-discovery and spiritual enlightenment. Therefore, the Wisdom Texts are important scriptures on the subject of human nature, spiritual psychology and mystical philosophy. The teachings presented in the Wisdom Texts form the foundation of religion as well as the guidelines for conducting the affairs of every area of social interaction including commerce, education, the army, marriage, and especially the legal system. These texts were sources for the famous 42 Precepts of Maat of the Pert M Heru (Book of the Dead), essential regulations of good conduct to develop virtue and purity in order to attain higher consciousness and immortality after death. ISBN1-884564-65-8    $18.95

## 48. THE KEMETIC TREE OF LIFE
**THE KEMETIC TREE OF LIFE: Newly Revealed Ancient Egyptian Cosmology and Metaphysics for Higher Consciousness** The Tree of Life is a roadmap of a journey which explains how Creation came into being and how it will end. It also explains what Creation is composed of and also what human beings are and what they are composed of. It also explains the process of Creation, how Creation develops, as well as who created Creation and where that entity may be found. It also explains how a human being may discover that entity and in so doing also discover the

ecrets of Creation, the meaning of life and the means to break free from the pathetic condition of human limitation and mortality in order to discover the higher realms of being by discovering the principles, the levels of existence that are beyond the simple physical and material aspects of life. This book contains color plates **ISBN: 1-884564-74-7** $27.95 U.S.

49. "Little Book of Neter" a summary of the most important teachings of Shetaut Neter (Ancient Egyptian religion) for all aspirants to have for easy reference **guide to the basic practices and fundamental teachings $3.00 (Soft) ISBN: 1-884564-58-5**

## 50. Dollar Crisis: The Collapse of Society and Redemption Through Ancient Egyptian Monetary Policy (Paperback)

by Muata Ashby  This book is about the problems of the US economy and the imminent collapse of the U.S. Dollar and its dire consequences for the US economy and the world. It is also about the corruption in government, economics and social order that led to this point. Also it is about survival, how to make it through this perhaps most trying period in the history of the United States. Also it is about the ancient wisdom of life that allowed an ancient civilization to grow beyond the destructive corruptions of ignorance and power so that the people of today may gain insight into the nature of their condition, how they got there and what needs to be done in order to salvage what is left and rebuild a society that is sustainable, beneficial and an example for all humanity. $18.99 u.s.

- **ISBN-10:** 1884564763
- **ISBN-13:** 978-1884564765

# Music Based on the Prt M Hru and other Kemetic Texts

Available on Compact Disc $14.99 and Audio Cassette $9.99

*Adorations to the Goddess*

**Music for Worship of the Goddess**

**NEW Egyptian Yoga Music CD**
**by Sehu Maa**
**Ancient Egyptian Music CD**
Instrumental Music played on reproductions of Ancient Egyptian Instruments– Ideal for <u>meditation</u> and
reflection on the Divine and for the practice of spiritual programs and <u>Yoga exercise sessions.</u>

©1999 By Muata Ashby
CD $14.99 –

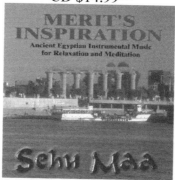

*MERIT'S INSPIRATION*
**NEW Egyptian Yoga Music CD**
**by Sehu Maa**

**Ancient Egyptian Music CD**
Instrumental Music played on
reproductions of Ancient Egyptian Instruments– Ideal for <u>meditation</u> and
reflection on the Divine and for the practice of spiritual programs and <u>Yoga exercise</u>
<u>sessions.</u>
©1999 By
Muata Ashby
CD $14.99 –
UPC# 761527100429

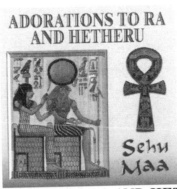

*ANORATIONS TO RA AND HETHERU*
**NEW Egyptian Yoga Music CD**
**By Sehu Maa (Muata Ashby)**
**Based on the Words of Power of Ra and HetHeru**
played on reproductions of Ancient Egyptian Instruments **Ancient Egyptian**
**Instruments used: Voice, Clapping, Nefer Lute, Tar Drum, Sistrums, Cymbals** –
The Chants, Devotions, Rhythms and Festive Songs Of the Neteru - Ideal for
meditation, and devotional singing and dancing.
©1999 By Muata Ashby
CD $14.99 –
UPC# 761527100221

### *SONGS TO ASAR ASET AND HERU*
**NEW**
**Egyptian Yoga Music CD**
**By Sehu Maa**

played on reproductions of Ancient Egyptian Instruments– The Chants, Devotions, Rhythms and Festive Songs Of the Neteru - Ideal for meditation, and devotional singing and dancing.

**Based on the Words of Power of Asar (Asar), Aset (Aset) and Heru (Heru)** Om Asar Aset Heru is the third in a series of musical explorations of the Kemetic (Ancient Egyptian) tradition of music. Its ideas are based on the Ancient Egyptian Religion of Asar, Aset and Heru and it is designed for listening, meditation and worship. ©1999 By Muata Ashby

CD $14.99 –
UPC# 761527100122

### *HAARI OM: ANCIENT EGYPT MEETS INDIA IN MUSIC*
**NEW Music CD**
**By Sehu Maa**

The Chants, Devotions, Rhythms and Festive Songs Of the Ancient Egypt and India, harmonized and played on reproductions of ancient instruments along with modern instruments and beats. Ideal for meditation, and devotional singing and dancing.

**Haari Om** is the fourth in a series of musical explorations of the Kemetic (Ancient Egyptian) and Indian traditions of music, chanting and devotional spiritual practice. Its ideas are based on the Ancient Egyptian Yoga spirituality and Indian Yoga spirituality.
©1999 By Muata Ashby
CD $14.99 –
UPC# 761527100528

### *RA AKHU: THE GLORIOUS LIGHT*
**NEW**
**Egyptian Yoga Music CD**
**By Sehu Maa**

The fifth collection of original music compositions based on the Teachings and Words of The Trinity, the God Asar and the Goddess Nebethet, the Divinity Aten, the God Heru, and the Special Meditation Hekau or Words of Power of Ra from the Ancient Egyptian Tomb of Seti I and more...

played on reproductions of Ancient Egyptian Instruments and modern instruments -
**Ancient Egyptian Instruments used: Voice, Clapping, Nefer Lute, Tar Drum, Sistrums, Cymbals**

— The Chants, Devotions, Rhythms and Festive Songs Of the Neteru – Ideal for meditation, and devotional singing and dancing.

©1999 By Muata Ashby
CD $14.99 –
UPC# 761527100825

### *GLORIES OF THE DIVINE MOTHER*
Based on the hieroglyphic text of the worship of Goddess Net.
**The Glories of The Great Mother**
©2000 Muata Ashby
CD $14.99 UPC# 761527101129`

## Order Form

Telephone orders: Call Toll Free: 1(305) 378-6253.  Have your AMEX, Optima, Visa or MasterCard ready
Fax orders: 1-(305) 378-6253     E-MAIL ADDRESS: Semayoga@aol.com
Postal Orders: Sema Institute of Yoga, P.O. Box 570459, Miami, Fl. 33257.  USA.
Please send the following books and / or tapes.

ITEM

_____Cost $_____
_____Cost $_____
_____Cost $_____
_____Cost $_____
_____Cost $_____
Total $_____

Name:_____

Physical Address:_____

City:_____ State:_____ Zip:_____

Sales tax: Please add 6.5% for books shipped to Florida addresses
_____Shipping: $6.50 for first book and .50¢ for each additional
_____Shipping: Outside US $5.00 for first book and $3.00 for each additional

_____Payment:_____
_____Check -Include Driver License #:

_____

_____Credit card: _____ Visa, _____ MasterCard, _____ Optima,
_____ AMEX.

Card number:_____
Name on card:_____ Exp. date:_____/_____

**Copyright 1995-2005 Dr. R. Muata Abhaya Ashby**
**Sema Institute of Yoga**
**P.O.Box 570459, Miami, Florida, 33257**
**(305) 378-6253 Fax: (305) 378-6253**